TRIUMPH
IN THE
DESERT

TRIUMPH
IN THE
DESERT

TEXT BY PETER DAVID

FOREWORD BY GENERAL COLIN L. POWELL
CHAIRMAN OF THE JOINT CHIEFS OF STAFF

EDITED BY RAY CAVE AND PAT RYAN

Contributions by
THE WORLD'S BEST PHOTOJOURNALISTS
AND ARTISTS OF THE U.S. ARMED FORCES

Additional text by
C.D.B. BRYAN   JOHN FIALKA   GREGORY JAYNES   MICHAEL KELLY   COLIN SMITH

Maps by
JOHN GRIMWADE

CENTURY
LONDON   SYDNEY   AUCKLAND   JOHANNESBURG

First published in the United Kingdom in 1991 by Century, an imprint of Random Century Group Ltd,
Random Century House, 20 Vauxhall Bridge Road, London SW1V 2SA

First published in the United States of America by Random House, Inc., New York, N.Y. 10022

Random Century Australia (Pty) Ltd, 20 Alfred Street, Milsons Point, Sydney, New South Wales 2061,
Australia

Random Century New Zealand Limited, 18 Poland Road, Glenfield, Auckland 10, New Zealand

Random Century South Africa (Pty) Ltd, PO Box 337, Bergvlei 2012, South Africa

Printed and bound in the United States of America

First Edition
A catalogue record for this book is available from the British Library

ISBN: 0 7126 5228 0

DEDICATED TO THOSE WHO GAVE THEIR LIVES

On September 14,
Powell rallied the crew
of the Wisconsin.

In Appreciation

General Colin L. Powell, Chairman of the Joint Chiefs of Staff

---- ✯ ----

Operation Desert Storm is now history. It was a mighty success for the cause of freedom in our world, for the United Nations, and for the United States. Most of all, it was a mighty success for the American people and their armed forces.

The most crucial of those forces were, of course, our troops in the field, the "thunder and lightning" of Desert Storm. The soldiers and sailors, the airmen and marines, the coastguardsmen—men and women, officers and enlisted, active and reserve—they performed simply superbly. They were not alone, however. Backing them all up were compatriots at home in the United States and around the world, the GIs and the civilians, who loaded, drove, flew, and sailed the wherewithal that was needed for victory in-theater.

And backing *them* up, in turn, were the teachers and trainers, and the designers and builders—in and out of uniform—whose toil over the past decade and more had yielded the finest strategists and tacticians, and the most effective weapons and equipment that the world of warfare has yet seen.

It didn't stop there. Families of our men and women in uniform were essential to their success, through their unselfish love and deep devotion. And the American people themselves—the heart and soul of our great democracy— through their extraordinary outpouring of support and help, gave to Operation Desert Storm the unstoppable momentum it needed to triumph.

The people—those of America and those of the international coalition to liberate Kuwait—are what our victory was all about. From the soldier in the desert threading his way through the mine fields, to the kid back home tying yellow ribbons to a tree, it was the people who accomplished this great task. They are our strength today and our hope for tomorrow.

As you page through this commemorative volume, I urge you to linger over the stunning photographs and telling descriptions of the people of Operation Desert Storm. Here on these pages are immortalized the images and the words of their heroic achievements. The people were the story. I laud them, I thank them, and I salute them.

On Target

A video eye with night vision, mounted in a bomb dropped from a French attack plane, sent back this evidence that an Iraqi munitions depot was destroyed.

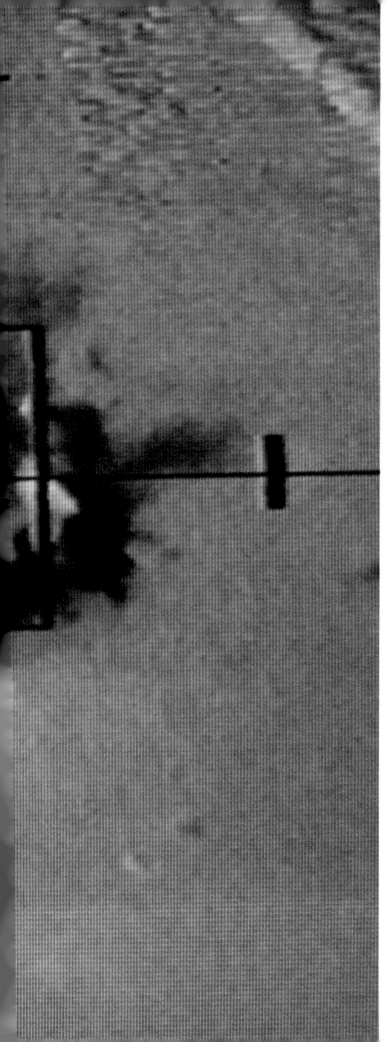

CONTENTS

One must never allow disorder to
continue so as to escape a war.
One does not escape: The war is merely
postponed to one's disadvantage.

MACHIAVELLI
THE PRINCE - 1514

Operation

Desert Storm

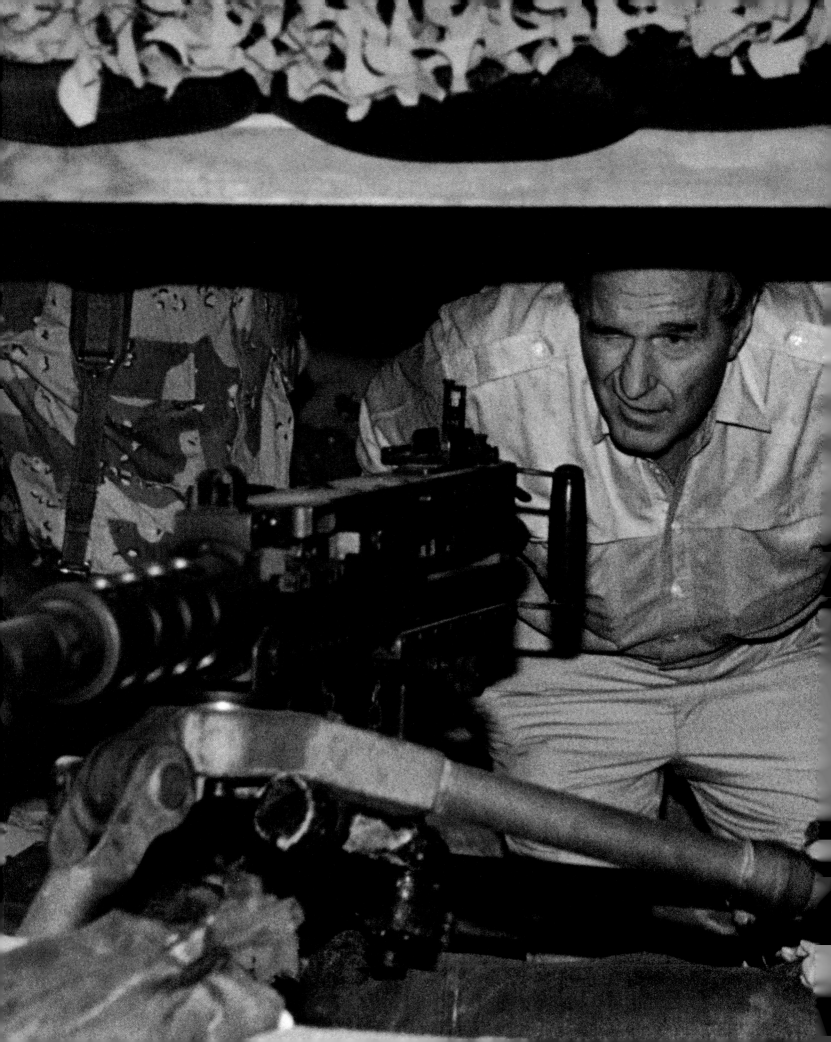

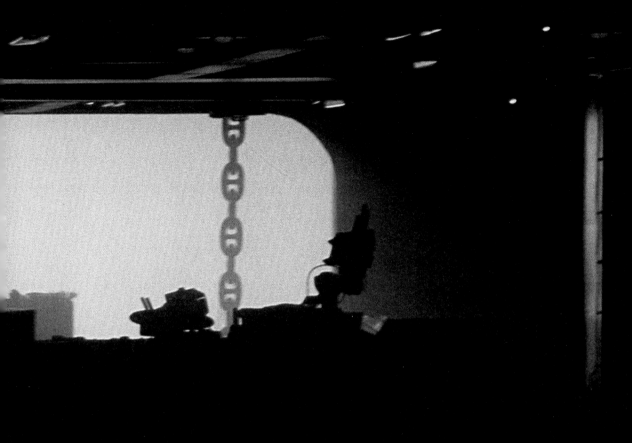

HOPE YOUR
VALENTINE'S DAY
IS JUST LIKE YOU!

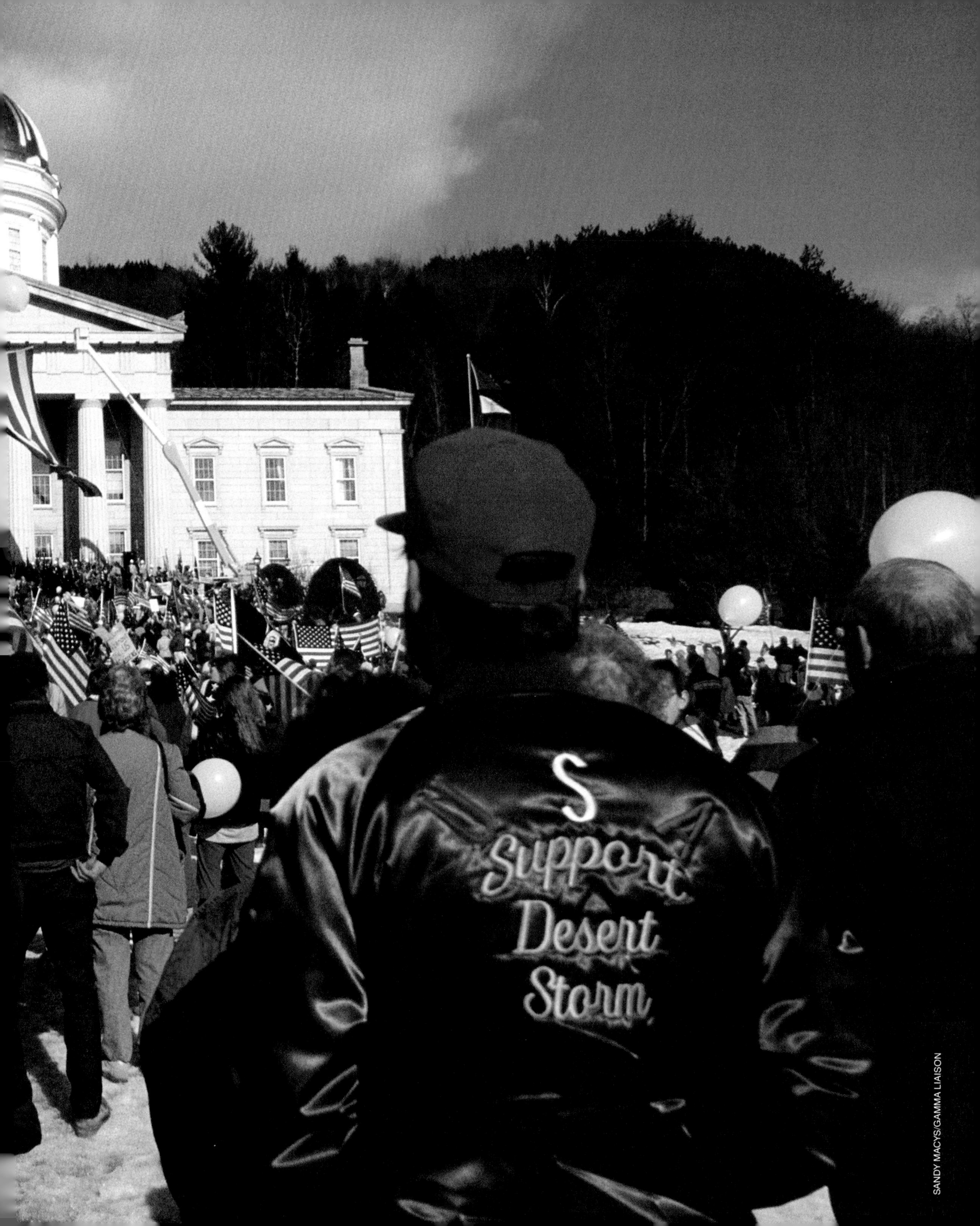

SANDY MACYS/GAMMA LIAISON

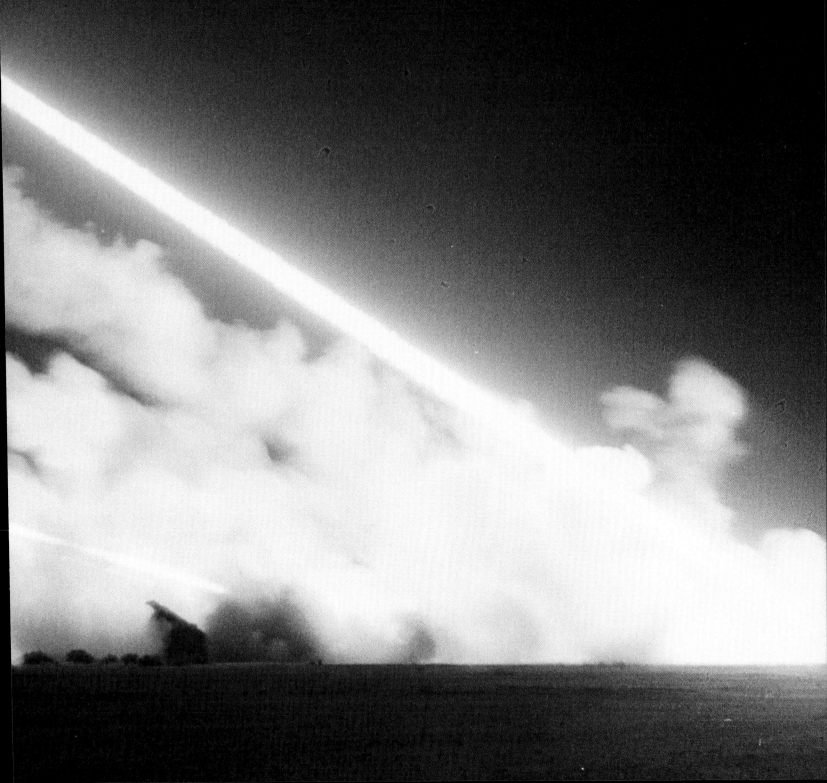

Operation Desert Storm

In the Saudi desert, AMX-30 battle tanks of France's armored 4th Regiment—a mobile attack force known as the French Dragons—prepare for the war.

On a Thanksgiving visit with marines at their base in Saudi Arabia, President Bush tours a bunker and sights down the barrel of a .50-caliber machine gun.

Logistical planners shipped billions of tons of supplies, including 2,000 tanks and 2,200 Bradley vehicles like these unloading near Dhahran.

In the midst of the five-month buildup of allied forces, soldiers of the U.S. Army's 1st Cavalry, marching to their posts, taste the dust of the desert.

Escaping the bloodshed of war for a moment, Amy Stuart, a nurse in the 5th Mobile Army Surgical Hospital, snoozes in her tent with a comforting friend.

An F/A-18 fighter-bomber, one of the 2,800 warplanes in the daunting allied aerial armada, takes wing from the carrier USS Midway.

Tracer shells etch a deadly web in the sky over Baghdad, as antiaircraft gunners fire blindly in search of Stealth fighters on bombing runs over the city.

Americans turned out at rallies across the nation, like this February gathering outside the state capitol in Montpelier, Vermont, to share their pride and prayers.

Aloft in their airborne office, General Colin Powell and Defense Secretary Richard Cheney head for the Gulf in early February to discuss final ground war plans.

As the ground war begins, U.S. artillery softens up Iraqi front lines with a barrage from MLRS mobile rocket launchers, firing a dozen missiles per minute.

Thick, greasy smoke rises from fires in Kuwait's Burgan oil fields. Iraq torched more than half the emirate's 1,000 wells: an environmental and economic disaster.

The low toll in allied casualties means little to this sergeant of the 24th Mechanized Infantry Division as he learns that friendly fire has killed his buddy. (Page 160)

Overwhelmed by the allies' lightning ground offensive, Iraqi soldiers south of Kuwait City emerged from their individual foxholes to surrender to Saudi troops.

Sabotaged oil wells blaze in the distance as U.S. soldiers in their Hummvee personnel carrier race through devastated landscape toward Kuwait City.

A father and son watch burning wells in the Ahmadi fields. About ten percent of the world's production was being destroyed in Kuwait each day.

Greeting POW Melissa Rathbun Nealy, held for thirty-two days, General Norman Schwarzkopf said, "I'd like to give you a hug. Do you mind?" She didn't.

TRIUMPH IN THE DESERT   33

Line in the Sand

---- ✯ ----

BY PETER DAVID

It is a quiet summer, and the world is not ready for Saddam Hussein's invasion

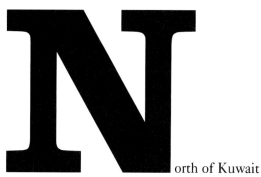

North of Kuwait City at a place called Mutla Ridge a caravan of death twisted north into the desert. This had been a chunk of the Iraqi army. Now it was a cemetery of burned-out trucks, tanks with blown-off turrets, stolen limousines shredded by cannon fire. In some of the trapped vehicles motors still idled. Others contained the corpses of Iraqi soldiers, cremated at their steering wheels as they tried to escape from the American bombers and attack helicopters. It reminded one journalist of a latter-day Pompeii.

This, though, was no natural disaster. It was the grisly result of a tragedy started six months earlier by a single man. On August 2, 1990, Saddam Hussein sent hundreds of his tanks streaming across Iraq's southern border into Kuwait, his next-door neighbor. The Kuwaitis, taken by surprise, never had a chance. Within twenty-four hours the invaders had seized control of government buildings, the international airport, the central bank, and the Emir's Dasman palace. The Emir himself, Sheik Jaber al-Ahmed al-Sabah, escaped to Saudi Arabia by helicopter. Sheik Fahd, his popular younger brother, was gunned down trying to defend the palace.

Saddam Hussein's excuse for what he had done changed from day to day. First he said the Kuwaiti people had risen up against their rulers. Then he said his army would withdraw once a new Kuwaiti government had been installed. Finally he annexed the place. Kuwait, he argued, had been carved out of what should have been Iraq by British colonialists and should never have existed. From now on the country that used to be Kuwait would be the nineteenth province of Iraq. It would stay that way forever, or Iraq would turn it into a "graveyard."

August's invasion fell upon a world that had been looking the other way. In the summer of 1990 America and the other Western democracies were still celebrating the end of the Cold War, the reunification of Germany, and the collapse of Eastern Europe's communist dictatorships. In Washington the talk on Capitol Hill was all about cuts in defense, about bringing American soldiers home from Europe and using the "peace dividend" to lift America out of recession. Wars of conquest launched by ruthless dictators were phantoms from the past. Had you told the average American back then that his country would soon be fighting the biggest war since Vietnam in the sands of Arabia he would probably have laughed in disbelief.

Saddam Hussein was banking on that disbelief. The Iraqi dictator had studied America's experience in Vietnam. What he read convinced him that the American people would no longer go to war unless their own heads were on the chopping block. Shortly before the invasion, he told the American ambassador in Baghdad that "yours is a society that cannot accept 10,000 dead in one battle." He had no such qualms. He had thrown away hundreds of thousands of his own people's lives in a futile war against Iran, and then called it a victory. From the presidential palace in Baghdad, the idea that the United States would risk a bloody war in the desert for the sake of liberating a tiny Middle Eastern emirate made no sense at all.

The world knows now that he was wrong. It didn't know it then, not even in the weeks after the invasion. Then, everybody wanted to believe that the nastiness in Kuwait was one of those passing summer clouds, which diplomacy would quickly dispel. Iraq, after all, was a small country, a third-world country. If the international community protested loudly enough, through the United Nations and the superpowers, Saddam Hussein would surely see that he had made a mistake and call his soldiers home. The international community did protest. Within hours of the invasion the United Nations Security Council demanded Iraq's immediate withdrawal. The United States sent an aircraft carrier, the *Independence*, from the Indian Ocean to the mouth of the Gulf. Yet Saddam Hussein did not budge. Slowly, the dimensions of the challenge in the Middle East began to sink in.

Despite being a small country, Iraq had built a vast war machine. Saddam Hussein could field an army of nearly a million men and some 5,000 battle tanks—nearly twice as many as all the tanks owned by Britain and France combined. His air force, the biggest in the Middle East, was equipped with the most modern French and Soviet combat aircraft. From the Soviet Union he had bought scores of ballistic missiles, and then extended their range so that they could reach Tel Aviv, Riyadh, and Tehran. He had made an enormous investment in chemical weapons, with which he had broken the spirit of Khomeini's army during the Iran-Iraq war. Expelling Iraq from Kuwait would be no mere police action, on the lines of America's interventions in Panama and Grenada. It would mean war on the scale of Vietnam or Korea.

Would such a war be worthwhile? Of course it would. A world in which one country got away with overrunning another just because it had an over-mighty army could never be at peace with itself. But, more than that, Saddam Hussein's invasion of Kuwait was a stark challenge to the vital interests of the modern democracies. Iraq possesses more oil than any country except Saudi Arabia. By invading Kuwait, Saddam Hussein almost doubled his reserves, putting a fifth of all the world's oil under his personal control. If he reached over the border and grabbed Saudi Arabia next, he would control 40 percent—nearly half—of the world's oil. Letting him get away with the invasion was unthinkable.

But so, many people argued back in August, was stopping him. That summery preinvasion world was not ready for Saddam Hussein. It had, in the glow of the end of the Cold War, chosen to forget that men like him still existed: men who ruled through terror in miserable countries untouched by the democratic idea. Nor, once it had remembered, was it sure that it could still muster the will to respond. George Bush, who had seen combat in Hitler's war, understood the perils of appeasement. The defining experience for many other Americans had been Vietnam. As far as they were concerned, foreign military entanglements could end only in defeat and shame.

And yet America did respond. Within days of the Iraqi invasion, the 82nd Airborne Division was pouring into Saudi Arabia to prevent further Iraqi aggression. While reinforcements steamed in by sea, these lightly armed paratroopers held a line in the sand, knowing they could be overrun by Saddam Hussein's tank divisions. Meanwhile the Iraqi dictator tried to turn his act of theft into something noble. He had invaded Kuwait, he said, so that he could liberate Palestine, help the poor against the rich, recover the honor of Islam. He called the coming war against the American-led alliance a *munazala*, a great duel between the righteous and the infidel. He would "chop off the heads of the evil-doers," make them "drown in their own blood." He promised to set the whole Middle East on fire and annihilate "the Zionist entity" with his chemical and biological weapons.

Looking back, it is hard to remember how many people believed him. Thousands of Muslims from Jordan to Bangladesh volunteered to fight for the thief who masqueraded as the new Saladin. And it was not only Muslims who fell under the spell. Before fighting began, while George Bush was still struggling to win the support of the United Nations and his own wavering Congress, many people in the West argued that anything, even appeasement, was better than the coming catastrophe. Edward Heath, a former British prime minister, said fighting Iraq could trigger the third world war. Saddam Hussein was "a very astute person, a clever person," with whom the world should be prepared to make a compromise. How foolish it all sounds now, in the shadow of that mangled convoy at Mutla Ridge. There was never anything noble or astute in Saddam Hussein's adventure; only greed, false pride, and overweening ambition. The Iraqi soldiers cut down from the sky as they fled from Kuwait with their plunder of television sets and luxury shoes died for nothing. They were as much the victims of their dictator's folly as were the Kuwaitis themselves.

The end of things, once witnessed, comes to seem inevitable. In the months after the liberation of Kuwait, the fears and doubts that preceded it slipped from the memory. Yet there was nothing easy or certain about the defeat of Saddam Hussein. De Tocqueville had long ago drawn attention to the difficulty all democracies confront in foreign policy:

"Foreign policy demands scarcely any of those qualities which are particular to a democracy; on the contrary it calls for the perfect use of almost all those qualities in which a democracy is deficient. Democracy is favorable to the increase of the internal resources of a state, it diffuses wealth and comfort...but it can only with great difficulty regulate the details of an important undertaking, persevere in a fixed design, and work out its execution in spite of serious obstacles. It cannot combine its measures with secrecy or await their consequences with patience. These are qualities which are more characteristic of an individual or an aristocracy."

Not always. Between the invasion of Kuwait and its liberation the United States raised a great international alliance, put Iraq under half a year of economic siege, and persuaded the United Nations to authorize the use of force if sanctions failed. It persevered in a fixed design, overcame serious obstacles, combined its measures with secrecy, and awaited their consequences with patience. The war, when it came, was brilliantly planned and courageously executed. But, although it ended in triumph, the result was not preordained. Saddam Hussein almost got away with his invasion of Kuwait.

Missing the Signals

How the chilling signs of aggression are misread as nervous bluster

For most of the world, waking up on August 2 to discover that Kuwait no longer existed, the invasion came like a bolt from the blue. Yet the surprise should not have been as total as it was. For the previous half-year Saddam Hussein had been showing signs of restlessness in foreign policy. For at least two months he had been grumbling in particular about the behavior of Kuwait, a country that Iraq had periodically claimed for itself. All of this should have alerted Western governments, and Iraq's Arab neighbors, to the danger brewing in the Gulf. It didn't, because in the first half of 1990 they were too distracted by the changes taking place in the Soviet Union and Eastern Europe. They were also too sure of their opinion that Iraq's exhausting war against Iran, which had ended only two years earlier, had turned Saddam Hussein into the sort of pragmatic leader the West could do business with.

It should not have taken the invasion of Kuwait to persuade the world that Saddam Hussein was an unusually bloodstained dictator. Modern Iraq has always been one of the world's violent places. Hemmed in by bigger neighbors (Turkey and Iran), lacking secure access to the waters of the Gulf, it nurses a strong sense of grievance and beleaguerment. The fear of outsiders is sharpened by the country's internal divisions. Like many of the modern Arab states that Britain and France created from the wreckage of the Ottoman empire, Iraq has bitter sectarian divisions. Although more than half of its eighteen million or so people belong to the Shiite stream of Islam, the government is largely in the hands of Sunni Muslims, who form less than a quarter of the population. Another quarter is made up of Kurds, a persecuted minority people who speak their own language and have tried many times to break free from Iraq altogether.

Even Iraqis acknowledge that holding this disunited nation together requires a strong central government. Since 1979, when Saddam Hussein became president, Iraq has had something worse: brutal, outright dictatorship. Saddam started his career as a small-town thug who threw in his lot with Iraq's Baath Socialist party. In 1959 he was part of a murder squad that wounded but failed to kill

the president of the day, Abdul-Karim Qassim. When Qassim was at last overthrown, in 1963, Saddam rose swiftly through the party's ranks, as an accomplished assassin and torturer. In 1968 a Baathist coup brought his cousin, Ahmad Hassan al-Bakr, to power, with Saddam as the powerful deputy in charge of internal security. By the time Saddam made himself president, eleven years later, he had already succeeded in building the apparatus of a ruthless police state.

It has become fashionable, since Iraq's invasion of Kuwait, to accuse Western governments of helping to put and keep Saddam Hussein in power. The charge is unfair. Like the Baath party itself, the Saddam Hussein of the 1970s was stridently anti-Western and anti-Israeli. When Egypt made peace with Israel in 1979, he joined Syria in leading the "rejectionist front" of Arab states which evicted Egypt from the Arab League. Baghdad became home to some of the most murderous Palestinian terrorist groups, like the one led by Abu Nidal. Saddam Hussein heaped scorn on the "conservative" Arab monarchies, such as Saudi Arabia and Jordan, that enjoyed good relations with the West. As a result, his relations with the United States and other Western governments were generally cool. Most of Iraq's modern weapons, and advice on how to use them, came from the Soviet Union.

The cozying up to the West did not begin until 1980, when Saddam Hussein launched an invasion against Iran, his bigger neighbor to the east. From Washington's point of view, neither regime seemed particularly appetizing. But it was Iran, under the fiery Ayatollah Khomeini, that appeared to pose the bigger threat to American interests in the Gulf. Gradually, as Saddam's invasion bogged down and his armies were pushed into reverse, he began

to turn westward for help. Eventually, the United States responded. Iraq, after all, was a secular country that had started toning down its anti-Western propaganda. If Iraq collapsed, Iran's Islamic revolutionaries might sweep on into the Arabian peninsula, knocking aside friendly regimes in Kuwait and Saudi Arabia and bringing the region's oil, on which the whole world depended, under the control of Ayatollah Khomeini.

This was the reasoning that led, in the late 1980s, to President Reagan's decision to "tilt" American policy Iraq's way in the Iran-Iraq war. At the time, Iran looked, misleadingly, as if it might win the war. The fanatical soldiers of its Revolutionary Guard and the fearless teenagers of its *Basij* volunteer corps were closing in on the Iraqi city of Basra. Iranian aircraft and gunboats were meanwhile attacking Kuwaiti oil tankers in the Gulf. At Kuwait's request, President Reagan agreed to reflag some of these tankers with the Stars and Stripes, and provide them with an escort of American warships. The Americans shared intelligence information with the Iraqis. There followed several clashes between the American and Iranian navies, and, in July 1988, the accidental shooting down by an American ship, the *Vincennes*, of an Iranian airliner packed with civilians. Within a month of that incident the eight-year Iran-Iraq war was over, with the Iraqis looking more like victors than the Iranians.

The history of the Iran-Iraq war, and the manner of its ending, appeared to establish a new relationship between the United States and Iraq. Fleetingly, in the dark shadow cast by Ayatollah Khomeini, their interests came together. But the Iran-Iraq war also planted the seeds of a fatal misunderstanding between the two countries. The Americans and the Iraqis emerged from the Iran-Iraq war with utterly different perceptions of what had happened in the course of it. Within two years this misunderstanding sprouted into Saddam Hussein's invasion of Kuwait.

As far as the United States was concerned, the Iran-Iraq war could hardly have ended in a more satisfactory manner. With its economy ravaged and its army exhausted, Iran was no longer a serious threat to its neighbors. After the death of Khomeini, a calmer and more pragmatic leader, Hashemi Rafsanjani, had taken over as president. Moreover, on the other side of the border, the war had apparently produced a gentler sort of Iraq. Saddam Hussein, once the West's implacable foe, had in American eyes been saved by the U.S. navy's intervention. He was no longer calling for the violent liberation of Palestine and had mended Iraq's relations with Egypt, the one Arab country to have made peace with Israel. In 1989 his decision to join together with Egypt,

THE MIDDLE EAST

BLACK SEA

U.S.S.R.

CASPIAN SEA

MEDITERRANEAN SEA

TURKEY

- Ankara

- Incirlik

SYRIA

- Kirkuk

- Beirut
- Damascus

LEBANON
- Haifa
- Tel Aviv

ISRAEL
- Amman
- Jerusalem

JORDAN

- Cairo

EGYPT

- Aqaba

- Al-Fallujah
- Samarra
- Baghdad

IRAQ

- Basra
- Bubiyan Island

- Tehran

IRAN

KUWAIT
- Kuwait City
- Khafji

RED SEA

- Medina

- Jubail
- Damman
- Dhahran

PERSIAN GULF

BAHRAIN

- Riyadh

QATAR
- Doha

- Jedda
- Mecca

SAUDI ARABIA

UNITED ARAB EMIRATES

- Abu Dhabi

- Masqat

OMAN

- Sana

YEMEN

ARABIAN SEA

GULF OF ADEN

Oil pipelines
Capital cities

Jordan, and North Yemen in a new regional association—the Arab Cooperation Council—seemed to confirm his coming of age as a moderate and a good neighbor.

That, at any rate, was the American view. As it turned out, Saddam Hussein saw things a little differently. Far from being grateful to the United States, he felt that the Americans, and his fellow Arabs, owed him a debt of gratitude after the ferocious war. In Saddam's eyes it was the sacrifices of his soldiers, and his military virtuosity, that had defeated the Iranians, not the help he received belatedly from the West. Even after victory he remained bitter over the Irangate affair, the Reagan administration's ill-starred attempt to buy the freedom of American hostages in Lebanon by giving arms to Ayatollah Khomeini. As for becoming a moderate on the Palestine issue, that had been a convenient way to win friends in the American Congress at a time when he needed them. Now that the fight against the Persian enemy was over he had an entirely new agenda to think about.

The Iran-Iraq war ended in the summer of 1988. Saddam Hussein invaded Kuwait exactly two years later. Should anything that happened in the intervening two years have tipped the world off? The clues were certainly there, had anyone been bothering to look. One was Iraq's

ARTISTS AT WAR

The U.S. military sent artists as well as arms to the desert, and a glimpse of their battlefront work appears on the pages of this narrative. Why not photographs? The armed services use cameras to gather intelligence and collect photographs more for "evidence" than evocation. It is part of a tradition officially begun in World War I. Former General Douglas Kinnard, chief of military history, says the U.S. war collection maintained by the Army Center of Military History in Washington, D.C. offers "valuable and memorable insights of the military heritage of America." The watercolors here are by Sergeant First Class Peter Varisano and Specialist First Class Sieger Hartgers of the army and Lieutenant Commander John Roach of the navy.

failure to demobilize its army. Despite the end of the war, up to a million men were kept under arms. Then there was the relentless quest to strengthen Iraq's military arsenal, despite the blunting of the Iranian threat. Between 1988 and 1990 Iraq spent billions of dollars on new weapons, including Scud missiles, new tanks, and the latest MiG-29 fighters. The Iraqis worked feverishly on ways to improve their chemical weapons, build a "supergun," and acquire nuclear arms. But the really incriminating clues only started to flow about six months before the invasion. Consider, for example, what happened in Jordan's capital, Amman, in February 1990.

That February was the first birthday of the Arab Cooperation Council, the new regional organization that so many Iraq-watchers in the West had taken as evidence of Saddam Hussein's intention to give up foreign adventures and become a good neighbor. The anniversary celebration was to be held in Jordan, with King Hussein as the host. For Jordan, the smallest member of the organization, the arrival of two of the Arab world's most important leaders—Iraq's Saddam Hussein and Egypt's Hosni Mubarak—was a significant event. King Hussein met his guests in person at the airport, showered them with kisses, and marched them one at a time past a guard of honor. The party, it seemed, was getting off to a good start.

Yet it ended badly, a day earlier than planned. Why? Ostensibly several of the participants had pressing business elsewhere. The real reason, however, was a speech delivered by Saddam Hussein on February 24 and broadcast on Jordanian television. In the speech, Hussein sought to analyze the great changes taking place in the world, and the impact that these changes were likely to have on the Middle East. The speech shocked and angered Mubarak. Its unexpected centerpiece was a vitriolic attack on the United States, the country that gives Egypt several billion dollars a year of vital aid.

Hussein's main focus in the speech was the waning power of the Soviet Union, which had for so long been Iraq's ally. Because of the Soviet decline, he said, the United States would over the coming five years emerge as the dominant power in the region. It would use this new power to hurt the Arabs. Indeed, it had already done so, by helping Soviet Jews emigrate to Israel. Another sign of America's evil intentions toward the Arabs was that it had kept warships on patrol in the Persian Gulf even though the Iran-Iraq war was long over. All this, the Iraqi leader told his listeners, was clear evidence of an American plot to dominate the Arab world and control its oil:

"The country that will have the greatest influence in the region, through the Arab Gulf and its oil, will maintain its superiority as a superpower without an equal to compete with it. This means that if the Gulf people, along with all Arabs, are not careful the Arab Gulf region will be governed by the interests of the United States...[Oil] prices would be fixed in line with a special perspective benefiting American interests and ignoring the interests of others."

The strident anti-Americanism of this speech—which included a call to reactivate the Arabs' "oil weapon" against Western interests—was not only unexpected. It was also a worrying throwback to the bad old Saddam Hussein of the 1970s, the radical Arab leader who in those days had delighted in denouncing the West and all its doings. And, by calling on America to pull its warships out of the Gulf, it was also a clear hint that Iraq's president still aspired to master the whole Gulf region himself. According to some reports, he also announced during a private session of the Amman meeting that Iraq was desperately short of money. Iraq, he said, had defended the rest of the Arab world from the Iranians. Now he expected Saudi Arabia and the other Gulf Arabs to give him $30 billion on top of the loans they had already made during that war.

All of this should have set some alarm bells ringing. Yet there is no evidence of any foreign governments other than Egypt's paying close attention to the contents of the Amman speech. In Western capitals, most foreign-policy experts assumed that the speech was just another burst of Iraqi paranoia, and would soon pass. After all, it was argued, Saddam had been coming under strong foreign criticism for his increasingly savage treatment of Iraq's Kurdish minority. There had been some talk in the American Congress of imposing sanctions, and the Voice of America had recently broadcast a commentary criticizing Iraq's secret police. In the U.S. State Department and Britain's Foreign Office the outburst in Amman was interpreted as an indication of ruffled feelings, not a hint of a surprise to come.

Then, less than two months later, came another ominous speech. On April 2, Saddam Hussein proudly announced to his people that Iraqi scientists had developed advanced "binary" chemical weapons—a type of weapon which had hitherto never been built in the third world. In itself, the announcement was not much of a surprise. Chemical weapons had served Iraq well in the war against Iran, and it was an open secret that its scientists were doing their best to make them more efficient. The surprise came in the tail end of the speech. "By God," Saddam suddenly declared, "we will make the fire eat up half of Israel if it tries to do anything against Iraq."

This time the rest of the world had to take notice. The United States, as Israel's closest ally, could hardly ignore an apparently unprovoked threat to half-annihilate the Jewish state. A State Department spokesman called the threat "inflammatory, outrageous and irresponsible." Yet, behind closed doors, the State Department continued to feel relaxed about Saddam. This latest outburst, analysts argued, was just another sign of nervousness. A month earlier, they pointed out, Iraq had executed Farzad Bazoft, a journalist from the London *Observer*, on a charge of being an Israeli spy. A little later British and American customs agents had thwarted an Iraqi attempt to smuggle special electrical switches, which could be used in making an atomic bomb, through London's Heathrow airport. These events had brought strong criticism of Iraq in Western newspapers. Perhaps, the analysts concluded, the Iraqi intelligence services had interpreted all these events as preparation for an Israeli attack, similar to its attack on Iraq's nuclear reactor in 1981. So once again the professional Iraq-watchers read Saddam's threats as nervous bluster, rather than a chilling signal of his true intentions.

While Western observers were playing down the impact of Saddam's threat against Israel, however, the rest of the Arab world seemed intent on playing it up. The oral rebuke issued by the State Department was promptly drowned out by the ecstatic response Saddam Hussein's latest speech received in most neighboring Arab capitals. There, the bloodcurdling threats against Israel turned the Iraqi leader into an instant hero. Even the Syrians, Iraq's bitterest rivals in the Arab world, were reluctantly impressed. From Damascus, President Hafez al-Assad said that the Arabs ought to bury their differences when it came to confronting the Zionist enemy.

Most Arabs were thrilled by the emergence of a strong Arab leader willing at last to defy Israel and with the military might to put his words into action. For the previous two years they had looked on helplessly as Israel used tough measures to put down the *intifada*, the civil uprising by the Palestinians in the Israeli-occupied West Bank and Gaza. At the same time, tens of thousands of Soviet Jews had begun to flock into Israel, some of them settling in the occupied territories. Vehement Arab protests in Moscow and Washington had done nothing to stem the immigration. Yet now, it seemed, the Arabs had a champion, armed to the hilt with missiles and chemical weapons, whom the world would have to listen to. Sheik Abdul-Hamid al-Sayeh, speaker of the Palestine National Council, the parliament of Yasser Arafat's Palestine Liberation Organization, captured the wider Arab mood. "We hail President Hussein," he said, "for his great speech, which represents his confidence in himself and in the strength of the Iraqi army, on which we still pin great hope for liberating Palestine."

To emphasize Arab support for Saddam, the Arab League decided to organize an emergency summit meeting in Baghdad at the end of May. "Our strength is in unity, our weakness in division," proclaimed the banners that went up all over the city as the heads of state arrived. The unity, though, was skin-deep. The meeting immediately exposed a deep rift between the Iraqis and Egyptians. Saddam Hussein's speeches were now larded with old-style anti-American slogans. He launched a ferocious attack on "American imperialism" and its support for "the Zionist enemy." Hosni Mubarak, in contrast, strove to cool passions, imploring his Arab brothers to send the outside world "a sensible message, in tune with the values and spirit of the age" rather than "a mere expression of anger." So far as the Arab-in-the-street could tell, what was happening in Baghdad was a titanic struggle between two powerful Arab leaders with opposite views about how to deal with the Israeli problem.

Or so it seemed. What really happened in Baghdad was quite different. The imagined danger from Israel may have filled Saddam Hussein's public speeches. In the private sessions, however, he was focusing his anger not on Israel to the west but on the Arab Gulf states to the south. He complained again, as he had in Amman in February, about the failure of these rich Gulf sheikdoms to write off the loans they had made to Iraq during the war against Iran. Some of them, he said, were waging a form of "economic warfare" against Iraq, by pumping out more oil than they were allowed to under the quotas set by OPEC, the Organization of Petroleum Exporting Countries. Their overproduction was pushing down the price of oil, and so reducing Iraq's income. Every dollar off a barrel of oil, he claimed, cost Iraq a billion dollars in badly needed revenues.

By now, the idea that Saddam Hussein had emerged wiser and more cautious from his war with Iran should have disappeared. All the evidence—his attack on America in Amman, his threats toward Israel, and his anger with the Gulf Arabs—suggested that he was once again a menace to the safety of the region. He had even begun to meddle in Lebanon, sending arms to the Christian warlord, General Michel Aoun, who was challenging the Syrians there. Yet there was still little appetite, in America or the Arab world, for picking a fight with him. The State Department had of course called his threats against Israel in April "outrageous." Even so, a few days later, Saddam was receiving a much softer message from the United States, via a party of American senators headed by the Republican minority leader, Robert Dole.

The senators met Hussein at the northern Iraqi city of Mosul, where they handed over a letter criticizing his attempts to acquire chemical and nuclear weapons. An

Iraqi transcript of the meeting, however, suggests that their main interest was in appeasing the dictator. Senator Dole represents Kansas, a big exporter of grain to Iraq. He told Saddam that a Voice of America journalist who was responsible for a broadcast comparing the Iraqi leader to Romania's former dictator, Nicolae Ceausescu, had been sacked. Alan Simpson, a senator from Wyoming, said that Hussein's problems were not with America's people but with its "haughty and pampered" press. The senators did not speak for the Bush administration. However, back in Washington, the administration was meanwhile fighting off efforts in Congress to impose economic sanctions on Iraq. John Kelly, assistant secretary of state for Near Eastern and South Asian affairs, conceded in hearings on Capitol Hill that events since February had "raised new questions about Iraqi intentions in the region." But imposing sanctions, he argued, would impair America's ability to exert "a restraining influence" on Iraq.

July 17 is Revolution Day in Iraq. It marks the anniversary of the Baath party's accession to power and it is one of the most important dates in the state calendar. On that day in 1990, Saddam Hussein finally brought his grievances against Kuwait and the United Arab Emirates out into the open. In a blistering television speech he accused them of plotting to undermine Iraq after its great military victory against Iran. They had, he said, "stabbed Iraq in the back with a poisoned dagger." He called the overproduction of oil, which had pushed down the price, "a large-scale, premeditated campaign by imperialist and Zionist circles against Iraq and the Arab nation." As for the Gulf states, "instead of rewarding Iraq, which sacrificed the blossoms of its youth in the war to protect their houses of wealth, they are severely harming it." If words failed to protect Iraq from this conspiracy, he warned his listeners, "we will have no choice but to resort to effective action to put things right."

This time there could be no doubting the danger. Iraq's foreign minister, Tariq Aziz, had sent a long list of written accusations to the Arab League, timed to coincide with Saddam's speech. The letter accused Kuwait of building military installations on Iraqi territory in 1980 and stealing oil worth $2.4 billion from the Iraqi part of the Rumaila oil field, which straddles the border between the two countries. Taken together, the letter and the speech terrified Sheik Jaber al-Ahmed al-Sabah, Kuwait's Emir. Kuwait's newly elected parliament was summoned into emergency session, Kuwaiti diplomats hurried abroad to gather up support. Their first port of call was Saudi Arabia, Kuwait's traditional ally and the strongest member of the six-country Gulf Cooperation Council, of which Kuwait was a member. In theory, all the countries of the council had undertaken to come to the defense of any member-state facing aggression. And yet in Saudi Arabia and elsewhere the Kuwaitis received a frosty welcome.

The reason was oil. Although Saudi Arabia had long been wary of Iraq, the regional superpower to the north, it shared Iraq's irritation with Kuwait's habit of ignoring its OPEC quota. Indeed, officials in Riyadh, the Saudi capital, did not believe that Iraq's verbal attacks against Kuwait amounted to a real threat of invasion. Like some of Kuwait's own ministers, they assumed that Saddam Hussein's intention was merely to scare the Kuwaitis into cutting oil production so that the oil price could rise. He might also, the Saudis conceded, want some other things: forgiveness of the $10 billion loan Kuwait had given him during the Iran war, for example, or a foothold on the Kuwaiti offshore islands of Warba and Bubiyan that would give Iraq a much-desired deep water port on the Gulf. But nobody in Saudi Arabia considered a full-fledged military invasion of Kuwait likely.

Oddly, or perhaps because they dared not believe otherwise, the Saudis clung to this view even after July 24, when American intelligence revealed that Iraq had moved 30,000 of its troops—enough, on their own, to outnumber the whole of the emirate's army—up to the Kuwaiti border. The troop movements sent a new ripple of concern through the Middle East. Egypt's President Mubarak offered his good offices as a mediator between the two "Arab brothers." The temptation to dismiss the Iraqi maneuvers as just another bout of saber-rattling persisted. After all, the American State Department reasoned, OPEC was due to hold an important meeting in Geneva only a few days later, and Iraq was clearly desperate to stop Kuwaiti quota-busting. If the Kuwaitis swallowed their pride in Geneva, the Iraqi troops would no doubt be withdrawn to their bases. Still, just to be on the safe side, the Americans decided to send a warning signal to Baghdad. Several American warships, it was announced, were to hold naval exercises with warships from the United Arab Emirates, lower down the Gulf.

On the same day, President Mubarak flew to Baghdad

to see if he could help to soothe tempers. The argument between Iraq and Kuwait was, he considered, nothing more than "a passing cloud." After meeting Saddam Hussein he went on to Kuwait, where he gave a cheerful press conference. The Iraqi president, he told reporters, had given a promise that no additional troops were stationed on the Kuwaiti border, and that the small number of troops there formed a permanent garrison. "I can tell you," he declared, "that President Saddam has no intention of sending his forces into Kuwait." By all accounts, Mubarak's main worry at this stage was not so much that Iraq might invade Kuwait but that the United States might add to the tension in the Gulf by overreacting. He urged the Americans to avoid any step that might be construed in Baghdad as escalation.

The Egyptian president need not have worried. In Washington, the State Department had evidently decided that its best approach to the growing crisis was to treat Saddam Hussein gently. The American naval exercise in the Gulf, it is true, had sent a faint warning. The State Department's spokesman had also announced, in response to Iraq's troop movements, that there was "no place for coercion and intimidation" in a civilized world. But the impact of these strong words was blunted by a confusing rider. The United States, said the State Department, "does not have any defense treaties with Kuwait, and there are no special defense or security commitments to Kuwait."

On July 25, when the American ambassador in Baghdad was summoned to meet the Iraqi president, Saddam Hussein was to receive an even fuzzier message from the Americans. It was this interview, many believe, that gave him the courage to go ahead with the invasion.

The American ambassador, April Glaspie, was a professional, seasoned diplomat who spoke fluent Arabic. A transcript of her interview with Saddam Hussein was later released by the Iraqis. According to Glaspie, this transcript was edited to the point of inaccuracy. She claims she warned the Iraqi dictator not to make the mistake of invading Kuwait, pointing out that the United States was a superpower and intended to act like one. None of this is contained in the Iraqi version of the meeting. Even so, the transcript shows the special difficulties many other diplomats would later

encounter when they tried to have a conversation with Saddam Hussein. The interview had barely begun before the Iraqi president launched into an angry, rambling presentation of Iraq's many complaints, most of which boiled down to a powerful sense of injustice.

Iraq, he insisted, had defended American interests by defeating Iran. Instead of being grateful, the Americans had conspired against Iraq during the Irangate affair. Even when that was over—once he had accepted Ronald Reagan's "apology"—the Americans had supported Iraq's enemies in Israel, Kuwait, and the United Arab Emirates. Now Hussein felt that he was the victim of another conspiracy. The "official American media" had started a campaign against him, and Kuwait was waging an economic war by deliberately pushing down the price of oil. "You know you are not the ones who protected your friends during the war with Iran," he went on. "Had the Iranians overrun the region, the American troops would not have stopped them, except by the use of nuclear weapons. I do not belittle you. But I hold this view by looking at the geography and nature of American society. Yours is a society which cannot accept 10,000 dead in one battle."

The Iraqi transcript shows Ambassador Glaspie trying to staunch this flow of invective by emphasizing the United States's continuing interest in good relations. She praised Iraq's postwar rebuilding efforts and expressed sympathy for its desire for a higher oil price. She said that the United States took no position on Iraq's territorial dispute with Kuwait, although (a detail not included in the Iraqi transcript) it did not want the dispute settled by force. President Bush was "an intelligent man" who did not wish to have an economic war with Iraq. Then, eventually, she steered the interview around to her main worry. What, she asked ("in the spirit of friendship, not of confrontation"), was the purpose of the Iraqi troop concentrations on the Kuwaiti border?

This set off another lecture. Hussein detailed the various peaceful ways in which he had tried to persuade the Kuwaitis to cut back their oil production, and the various perfidious means by which they had thwarted him. Then he dropped some news. President Mubarak had just telephoned to set up direct talks between Iraq and Kuwait. This is how the conversation ended:

GLASPIE: Congratulations.
SADDAM: A protocol meeting will be held in Saudi Arabia. Then the meeting will be transferred to Baghdad for deeper discussion directly between Kuwait and Iraq. We hope we will reach some result.

We hope that the long-term view and the real interests will overcome Kuwaiti greed.

GLASPIE: May I ask when you expect Sheik Saad [Kuwait's crown prince] to come to Baghdad?

SADDAM: I suppose it would be on Saturday or Monday at the latest. I told brother Mubarak that the agreement should be in Baghdad Saturday or Sunday. You know that brother Mubarak's visits have always been a good omen.

GLASPIE: This is good news. Congratulations.

SADDAM: Brother President Mubarak told me they [the Kuwaitis] were scared. They said troops were only twenty kilometers north of the Arab League line. I said to him that regardless of what is there, whether they are police, border guards or army, and regardless of how many are there, and what they are doing, assure the Kuwaitis and give them our word that we are not going to do anything until we meet with them. When we meet and when we see that there is hope, then nothing will happen. But if we are unable to find a solution, then it will be natural that Iraq will not accept death, even though wisdom is above everything else. There you have the good news.

GLASPIE: I am planning to go to the United States next Monday. I hope I will meet with President Bush in Washington next week. I thought to postpone my trip because of the difficulties we are facing. But now I will fly on Monday.

Ambassador Glaspie clearly felt that the meeting had gone well; well enough at any rate for her to go ahead with plans to leave Baghdad and return to Washington. Her assumption may not have been wise, but it was not completely unreasonable either. Saddam Hussein had made it pretty clear that Iraq intended to drive a hard bargain with the Kuwaitis at the forthcoming OPEC meeting, due in a few days' time. It would expect the oil price to rise. But the chances of a military invasion of Kuwait, she thought, were negligible now that Saddam Hussein had given his word to President Mubarak that there would be no invasion while Iraq and Kuwait were still talking. Arrangements for those talks had been made. Everything she knew about the Arab code of honor and prudence suggested that the president of Iraq would not lightly break a personal promise given to the president of Egypt, the Arab world's most populous country. In other words, the crisis had been defused.

At first, events seemed to show that Ambassador Glaspie was right. Two days later, on July 27, OPEC's oil

ministers assembled in Geneva. To nobody's surprise, the Kuwaitis, with an Iraqi army camped menacingly on their border, agreed that it was time for them to cut oil production and let the price rise toward $21 a barrel. By arrangement with the Egyptians, this was to be followed by the pair of Iraqi-Kuwaiti meetings—one in Saudi Arabia and another in Iraq—Saddam had mentioned to Ambassador Glaspie. There the two sides would try to thrash out their differences on other disputes, including Iraq's border claims and its accusation that Kuwait had stolen Iraqi oil from the shared Rumaila field. In embassies and foreign ministries throughout the Middle East, diplomats assumed that the Kuwaitis would have no choice but to buy their way out of trouble. "The next few days will witness a complete improvement in relations," Egypt's foreign minister, Esmat Abdel Meguid, predicted gaily.

It was not to be. On August 1, one of Hussein's closest lieutenants, Izzat Ibrahim, traveled to the Saudi port of Jedda to start the talks with the Kuwaitis. They collapsed almost immediately, for reasons that are still a matter of dispute. The Iraqis say that the Kuwaiti delegation was unwilling to make any concessions at all. The Kuwaitis say that they offered to write off the Iraqi debt and lease Warba Island to Iraq, but that the Iraqis wanted Bubiyan too. Whatever the truth, Ibrahim flew home in a rage. The following morning, in the early hours of August 2, T-72 tanks of the Iraqi Republican Guard rolled across the border and blasted their way into Kuwait.

For half a year Saddam Hussein had been testing the response of the Americans to a series of increasingly provocative threats. Receiving no convincing counterthreat, he decided to swallow up his neighbor. Now America would have to decide what it was willing to do about it.

Magic at the U.N.

Twelve of the world's most powerful leaders take a call from George Bush

As luck would have it, George Bush had a guest with him on the day of the Iraqi invasion. Margaret Thatcher, then still Britain's prime minister, was visiting the President at a ranch in Aspen, Colorado. Eight years earlier, in 1982, she too had been caught unawares by an invasion, when Argentina launched a sudden attack on a British possession, the Falkland Islands. To the surprise of the world, and the dismay of Argentina's military rulers, she had reacted vigorously, sending a British armada halfway around the globe to wrest the islands back.

In Colorado, the President and the Prime Minister quickly agreed that the invasion of Kuwait could not be allowed to stand. But when they emerged from their private discussions to give a windswept open-air press conference, neither sounded enthusiastic about a military response. Earlier in the day, in New York, the Security Council had acted with unusual haste in passing a resolution calling on Iraq to withdraw "immediately and unconditionally" from Kuwait. President Bush had also frozen all Iraqi and Kuwaiti assets in the United States, and banned the import of Iraqi oil. Now the two leaders stressed the need for economic sanctions against Iraq, and the importance of all members of the United Nations, not just the Western powers, agreeing to support them. When he was questioned about the possible use of force, Bush was evasive. "I'm not contemplating such action and I would not discuss it even if I were," he replied.

That was Thursday, August 2. Bush spent the following anxious weekend with his advisers at Camp David. On his return to Washington, he seemed to have changed both his state of mind and his tone of voice. The initial glimmer of hesitation about standing up to Iraq had vanished without a trace. In a brief and sometimes prickly press conference on the White House lawn he told reporters he was absolutely determined to bring about a complete withdrawal of Iraqi forces from Kuwait. Nor was there any question of accepting the puppet regime the Iraqis were at that moment trying to install in Kuwait. "This will not stand," he said, "This will not stand, this aggression against Kuwait." Asked what he could do to prevent Iraq from installing a puppet regime, he snapped back: "Just wait. Watch and learn."

What had happened at Camp David to alter the President's mood? For one thing he had been in conclave with his military advisers. Those present included the secretary of defense, Dick Cheney, plus the chairman of the Joint Chiefs of Staff, General Colin Powell. Also consulted was the bearish chief of Central Command, a virtually unknown general named Norman Schwarzkopf. Both of these generals had acquired reputations as can-doers, in contrast to predecessors who had tended instinctively to advise against foreign military entanglements. But both had also served double tours in Vietnam and had brought home with them all of that war's psychological baggage. In particular, they were haunted by the fear that the American armed forces would once again be committed piecemeal, in inadequate numbers, to a political venture without clearly defined aims.

General Powell's attitude, then as later, was simple. He would do whatever the President asked of him, but would insist on being given all the forces he deemed necessary to complete the mission properly. Pushing the Iraqi army out of Kuwait, he told the President, would be a tremendous undertaking. Although American aircraft carriers were steaming for the Gulf, the United States had no land bases close to Kuwait. If it managed to acquire bases, it would still be a difficult feat to transport enough ground forces into them to pose a serious threat to Iraq's large and experienced tank army. And even setting up a defensive screen in Saudi Arabia would be fraught with dangers. At a minimum, that would require sending several divisions with heavy armor, plus a powerful air force contingent.

Yet, daunting as the task seemed, the Pentagon was not completely unprepared. The formal mission of General

Schwarzkopf's Central Command, with headquarters at MacDill Air Force Base in Tampa, Florida, was to be able to deploy American forces rapidly in an emergency. The command had begun life in the 1970s as President Jimmy Carter's "Rapid Deployment Force" (RDF). Since then it had gone through several changes of name and organization before becoming one of the main American operational commands, responsible directly to the secretary of defense and, through him, to the President. The eyes of Central Command had always been fixed on the Middle East. Without making light of the difficulties, General Schwarzkopf was able to reassure Bush that he had prepared a viable contingency plan that would enable the United States to intervene militarily in Kuwait if that was what the President decided to do.

In its old RDF days, the strategic nightmare the command spent most of its time worrying about was a Soviet armored attack across Iran toward the oil fields of the Gulf. At that time Iran, still under the Shah, was a close American ally. The RDF worked from the assumption that in the case of an all-out Soviet attack the Iranian forces would be destroyed early on, leaving the main job of defending the Gulf and its oil to the RDF itself. So plans were made for flying American combat aircraft rapidly into bases in friendly Arab countries such as Oman, Saudi Arabia or Kuwait. These countries, it was assumed, would want to cooperate to save themselves from being overrun by the Russians. But in case they did not, contingency plans were laid to establish makeshift air bases inside Iran itself.

Nobody at the Pentagon had any illusions about the difficulty of fighting at short notice in the Middle East. Under the RDF's plans, the combat aircraft would be followed within a matter of hours by two American airborne divisions: the 82nd, based at Fort Bragg in North Carolina, and the 101st, from Fort Campbell, Kentucky. The 82nd was mainly a parachute division; the 101st was a helicopter-intensive division, lavishly equipped with both troop-lifting choppers and specialized tank-busting gunships. Even so, these light forces were not judged to possess the firepower to stop a determined Soviet armored attack. The aircraft might take a heavy toll of Russian tanks strung out across the countryside. In the rugged Iranian mountains the paratroopers and special forces could hurt them some more. But this would be a delaying action at best. To stop the Russians and throw them back, some way had to be found to get heavier American equipment on the scene, and fast.

The only answer seemed to be pre-positioning. American forces located in the United States, but promised to NATO in time of war, had for a long time kept much of their heavy armor in stores in Germany. In an emergency the soldiers would fly across the Atlantic and marry up with their tanks in Germany. But the American planners soon concluded that pulling off the same stunt in the Middle East would be far more difficult. Given the political sensitivities of the region, hardly any governments were keen to act as willing hosts. Besides, nobody could be sure where a war in the Middle East would start. It might take weeks to load and ship equipment stored, say, in Oman, to the scene of a battle in Iran or Iraq.

The obvious solution to this conundrum was to store the equipment at sea. In the 1970s the RDF assembled a group of seven large merchant ships manned by civilian crews and anchored them at the American base of Diego Garcia in the Indian Ocean. They were loaded with enough materiel to equip an entire Marine Corps brigade (about 15,000 men, including an attached aircraft squadron) plus some fuel, water, bombs, and other stores for air force combat aircraft. From Diego Garcia the squadron would be able to steam to any port in the Gulf within a few days and join marines flown out from their home bases in the United States. Soon the system was deemed to work well enough for the Pentagon to enlarge this original

squadron. Eventually two more flotillas, known as maritime pre-positioning squadrons, were added.

By dint of these preparations, the United States had given itself the ability to move about three marine brigades, along with most of their equipment, into action within a few days of an emergency in the Gulf. But not even the marine divisions would stand a real chance of prevailing in a head-on confrontation with the Soviet Union's massive tank armies. To win such a war, the United States would have to bring some of its army heavy divisions to bear. These units had bigger and better tanks —generally the M1 Abrams instead of the marines' older M-60s—and more of them. They also had an enormous "tail" of supporting forces: trucks, air defenses, engineering support, and reconnaissance units. In Europe, where the vehicles could be stored ashore and where there was a massive logistics system already in place, pre-positioning the equipment for a few armored and mechanized divisions worked well. In the Gulf, the army's heavy divisions would have to come, bag and baggage, from the United States or Germany.

How? Moving the equipment by air was out of the question. For once, though, luck was on the planners' side. In the late seventies, eight large and fast (31-knots), roll-on-roll-off ships came on the market at a bargain price, and the navy bought them all, expressly so that they could be used to lift the heavy divisions from the United States, or perhaps Germany, to the Gulf or to other trouble spots. The ships were refurbished and anchored at various American ports on the Atlantic and in the Gulf of Mexico. On one occasion the loading of an entire brigade (belonging to the 24th Infantry Division) was practiced, but most of the time the ships rode empty at anchor, awaiting a rainy day. They were later to play a crucial part in Desert Shield, the operation to defend Saudi Arabia from an Iraqi attack.

Although Central Command was consulted about these developments, it was not involved directly. Indeed, Central Command had no permanent forces at all under its wing. Its only job was to make plans. Nevertheless, a number of formations were specially earmarked for rapid-deployment operations. General Schwarzkopf included them in his planning, and the relevant units conducted exercises designed to prepare them for the sort of brushfire operations Central Command had in mind. Among these forces were the marine brigades and their pre-positioned ships at Diego Garcia, several air force wings, the 82nd and 101st Airborne Divisions, the 24th Infantry Division (Mechanized) at Fort Stewart, Georgia, and the XVIII Corps headquarters, which was the parent command of the two airborne divisions.

Meanwhile, throughout the 1970s and 1980s, the army had been searching for ways to intervene powerfully in unexpected, faraway wars. Much effort went into finding new equipment for the airborne forces. Traditionally, the mission of airborne units had been to drop by parachute in an enemy's rear, disrupt his communications briefly during a critical period, and then join up with heavier units advancing overland. However, with the coming of the RDF concept, it was apparent that the airborne units might have to operate for extended periods on their own. This meant the paratroopers would need vehicles to move them around the battlefield once they had folded their parachutes. They would also need light armor: something light enough to transport by aircraft but potent enough to destroy pillboxes and thin-skinned vehicles, and capable at least of launching a decent antitank missile if it ran into the enemy's main armor.

The first requirement resulted in the development of the "dune buggy": a rugged and agile vehicle, looking like a cross between a jeep and a motorcycle, which could be mounted with a heavy machine gun and transport the paratroopers at high speed over all kinds of terrain. For armor, the airborne divisions turned to the Sheridan, a light reconnaissance tank mounting a 152mm gun that can be used either as a short-range cannon or as the launcher for an antitank missile with a shaped-charge warhead. The Sheridan was considerably inferior to the M1 Abrams, but it was air-transportable. The airborne soldiers liked it. They felt they could put up with the short range of its gun.

Against this background, the change in President Bush's tone once he returned from Camp David that first weekend becomes easier to understand. War with Iraq must still have struck the President as a remote and almost reckless option. On the home front, Americans were still struggling to come to terms with the invasion. Many were hearing for the first time about the existence of Saddam Hussein, and few had reason to care about the fate of faraway Kuwait. There was no public appetite for a military clash. On the other hand, the President had now been persuaded that, if he did pick up the gauntlet Saddam Hussein had thrown down, the United States was not bereft of a credible military option in the Gulf. One way or another, the President decided, Kuwait would be liberated. For the time being, though, the preferred method would be diplomacy, and economic blockade.

Economic sanctions, such as those imposed against South Africa, had never been popular with the Bush administration. They had seldom achieved their intended aims. This time, however, the President had reason to believe that they would have a fair chance of succeeding. He had spent a lot of time on the telephone at Camp David, talking directly to a dozen of the world's most powerful leaders, including Japan's Toshiki Kaifu, France's François Mitterrand, Germany's Helmut Kohl, Turkey's Turgut Ozal, Canada's Brian Mulroney and, of course, the indefatigable Mrs. Thatcher. These conversations appear to have convinced the President that, against Iraq, sanctions might stand a chance. For once, it seemed, the United States would be able to count on the strong support of friends if it chose to take tough action. And for once there was a particular economic measure that looked capable of achieving the desired result.

Over the weekend both Japan and Western Europe had followed America's lead, suspending purchases of Iraqi oil and freezing Iraqi and Kuwaiti assets. Iraq possesses huge reserves of oil—at 110 billion barrels the biggest in the world after Saudi Arabia. In the past, owning a lot of oil was considered to give a country political strength. But what if the oil weapon could be turned around and made to work in reverse? After all, if Americans and Europeans were addicted to buying oil, Iraqis were even more addicted to selling it. On the eve of the invasion, exports accounted for a staggering 95 percent of Iraq's foreign-currency earnings. Better still, Iraq was self-sufficient in virtually nothing else except for dates and grapes. Cut off its sales of oil and it would eventually run out of the money it needed to import food, machinery, and spare parts for its factories. But to achieve any of this, President Bush would first have to win the active cooperation of two particular foreign statesmen: King Fahd of Saudi Arabia and Turgut Ozal, the president of Turkey.

Iraq has only two efficient ways to get its oil to market: by tanker, through the Persian Gulf, or by overland pipelines across Turkey to the Mediterranean or across Saudi Arabia to the Red Sea. It would be a simple enough matter for the American navy to bottle up the sea-lanes through the Gulf. The question was whether the Turks and Saudis would agree to stop up their pipelines. For Turkey the decision would be relatively easy. Antagonizing Iraq would mean a financial sacrifice. Iraq's use of the pipeline earned Turkey a handsome $400 million a year. But Turkey was a member of NATO with a large and powerful army of its own. President Ozal could afford to irritate Saddam Hussein without running much risk of an Iraqi attack on his country. The Americans knew that talking the Saudis into cooperating was going to be a much tougher proposition.

For an oil embargo to work, the Saudis would have not

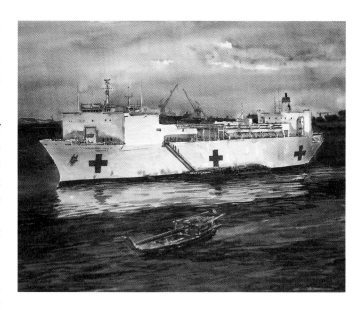

only to stop up Iraq's pipelines but also agree to pump a lot more of their own oil to make up for the world's losses from Iraq or Kuwait. Saudi help would also be essential, if later, there was to be any American military response in the Gulf. "It's a long ways away and it's a harsh climate," Admiral William Crowe, Jr., a former chairman of the Joint Chiefs of Staff, said on television shortly after the Iraqi invasion of Kuwait. "It's very difficult to reach and it requires some kind of local access. Now if we have that local access…then we can put force in there. We can draw a line. We can do whatever we want to if we have the political will." Saudi Arabia was the only place from which the Americans could realistically launch a war to rescue Kuwait. That is why the single most important decision President Bush reached at Camp David on the first weekend of the Gulf crisis was to send Dick Cheney to see King Fahd.

King Fahd had already been softened up by two long telephone conversations with Bush. Even so, Cheney knew his job would not be easy. Unlike the Turks, the Saudis were both weak and terrified. Saudi Arabia is one of the world's odder countries. A vast, empty place, it contains 20 percent of the world's oil reserves. It is governed benignly but autocratically by the ruling family, the al-Sauds, who united its warring tribes by conquest in the 1920s. Since then the ruling family's abiding aim has been to contrive ways of being left alone, so that it can enjoy its fabulous oil wealth without disturbance and preserve a way of life that is still largely tribal.

Over the years the Saudis had grown accustomed to the presence of millions of foreign workers, needed both to run the modern bits of their economy and do the menial jobs the Saudis would not do for themselves. But, in general, the government detested foreign influence, and the social disruption such influence might bring. As custodian of Mecca and Medina, the holiest places of Islam, King Fahd was uncomfortable about the presence of non-Muslims in his kingdom. In foreign policy the Saudi watchword had always been caution. The kingdom had developed a habit of using money to buy off potential threats from more powerful neighbors to the north. Like Kuwait, it had contributed generously to Iraq's war chest during the war against Iran. In normal times, the very idea of Saudi Arabia cooperating with the Americans against an Arab neighbor as dangerous as Saddam Hussein would have been laughed out of King Fahd's court.

These, though, were not normal times. The Saudis had welcomed Kuwait's humiliation at the OPEC meeting a few days earlier. But, like April Glaspie and almost everybody else, they were taken utterly by suprise when Iraqi tanks rumbled into Kuwait City. So shocked were they that the state-controlled media were told at first not to broadcast the news. Kuwait, after all, had been an ally, a fellow member of the Gulf Cooperation Council that included all of the six oil-rich monarchies of the Arabian peninsula. In principle, an attack on one member was to be considered an attack on all. The council had even

raised a joint army, the "Peninsula Shield Force," and based it at Hafar al-Batin, a small town in the northeast corner of Saudi Arabia. But neither this small force of several thousand men, nor Saudi Arabia's own armed forces of a little over 100,000, could hope to stand up against the might of Iraq.

When Cheney flew into Saudi Arabia on August 6 he therefore found King Fahd wavering between fury and fear. The king was furious at the sacking of Kuwait, but frightened that by complaining too loudly he would simply promote himself to the top of Saddam Hussein's hit list. Baghdad was already warning that closing the pipeline would be an act of war, and the king was excruciatingly aware of his country's vulnerability. The capital, Riyadh, was only a few hours' drive from the Iraqi border. And, if it chose to, Saddam's army had only to stretch out its hand to capture the kingdom's principal oil fields just south of Kuwait on the western shore of the Gulf. Could a man as ambitious as he resist the temptation?

In the end, the Iraqis might have made up King Fahd's mind for him. Publicly, Saddam Hussein claimed that he had no designs on Saudi Arabia, that his quarrel had been with Kuwait alone. But Secretary of Defense Cheney showed King Fahd satellite photographs that appeared to tell a different story. Iraq was not simply consolidating its hold on Kuwait but pouring thousands of extra troops into the captured emirate. Hundreds of Iraqi tanks had massed on the Saudi border. Some had reportedly infiltrated the so-called "neutral zone" between the two countries. All this suggested that King Fahd might face an invasion anyway, regardless of whether he cooperated with the Americans. Finally, fear helped him decide. He would close the pipeline—provided that the Americans would defend him from Iraqi military retaliation.

The Americans did not have to be asked twice. On August 7 the White House announced that Saudi Arabia was facing "imminent danger" and that American troops and combat aircraft were flying out to defend it. Within hours, paratroopers from the U.S. Army's elite 82nd Airborne Division were on their way, along with F-15 fighters from the air force. Operation Desert Shield was born. Saudi Arabia's own army, which had previously been staying out of sight, moved conspicuously out of its barracks and north toward the border. The previous day, the U.N. Security Council had clamped a far-reaching trade and financial embargo against Iraq. Saudi officials duly promised that Iraqi oil would stop flowing across Saudi territory, and that the kingdom would start pumping an extra two million barrels a day of its own oil to help make up the shortfall. On August 9 Britain joined the military effort, promising to send two squadrons of Tornado and Jaguar aircraft, amid rumors that two Arab countries—Egypt and Morocco—were thinking of contributing ground forces.

On Friday August 10, a week and a day after the invasion, President Bush decided against spending a second anxious weekend at Camp David. Instead, he went to his seaside home in Kennebunkport, Maine, for a long-planned holiday. "I think the American people want to see life go on," he explained. "What you don't want to do is appear to be held hostage in the White House." In truth there was little relaxation to be had at Kennebunkport: Virtually the whole emergency apparatus of the White House moved up to Maine with him. But the President could at least look back with satisfaction over a week that had seen an extraordinary reversal of fortunes. Saddam's invasion had taken America by surprise. And yet, by week's end, it was Iraq's president who looked as if he had been locked in a trap.

The Iraqi dictator had invaded Kuwait mainly in order to boost his revenues from oil. Now, thanks to the embargo, he was unable to sell any oil at all. With American and British troops and aircraft pouring into Saudi Arabia, the full scope of his blunder was beginning to dawn on him. He had known that invading Kuwait was a dangerous gamble and had expected the Americans to complain. He never foresaw that within days of the invasion a great American army and air force would be assembling in Saudi Arabia. Had he not hinted to April Glaspie that he might choose war if the negotiations with Kuwait failed? She had given no warning—presumably because she was not authorized to—that such an action would invite a military response. The vigor of the American action startled him, upsetting his preinvasion calculations. But he had also made two other miscalculations. One concerned the Arab reaction. The other concerned the Soviet Union.

Nobody outside Iraq knows for certain when Saddam Hussein first decided to invade Kuwait. But there are clear signs that he had begun to prepare for the reaction in the region well in advance. In 1989, for example, the Iraqi leader became an enthusiastic founding member of the Arab Cooperation Council, thereby strengthening his relationship with Egypt. He had recently signed a nonaggression pact with Saudi Arabia, a move that was probably designed to make the Saudis feel less alarmed about his subsequent invasion of their neighbor. And he had begun to put out peace feelers towards Iran's President Rafsanjani, hinting at Iraq's readiness to end the dispute between them over control of the Shatt al-Arab waterway and so turn their cease-fire into a peace. Squaring relations with his former victim on the east must have seemed a useful precaution before setting off on another land grab southward.

These precautions may have persuaded Hussein that the reaction to the invasion from his neighbors and near-neighbors would be muted. He could also count on several other factors. One was the unpopularity of the Kuwaitis, whom most Arabs from the poorer parts of the Middle East tended to regard as haughty, selfish, and undeservedly rich. Another was the high personal standing his recent defiance of Israel had won him in Arab opinion everywhere. But, even if he was wrong and his brother regimes did choose to object to the invasion, what could they do about it? Given that no Arab army was as mighty as his own, his neighbors would in the end have no choice but to accept a fait accompli.

And so it appeared to turn out—at first. Immediately after the invasion, the Saudi government's only reaction was to impose a news blackout. In Jordan, and among Palestinians everywhere, news of the invasion was greeted with delight, as yet another sign of their favorite Arab leader's strength and daring. Attempts by Egypt and Saudi Arabia to organize an emergency Arab summit in Jedda three days after the invasion collapsed because of objections from Libya and the Palestine Liberation Organization. A lot of Arab intellectuals argued that the Kuwaiti fat cats had richly deserved to be invaded by the country that had protected the Arabs against Iran in the Gulf war. "Is it right," intoned a columnist in the *Jordan Times*, "that Iraq should pay the bill not only in souls but in cash while Arab money is being invested, even squandered, in pursuit of luxuries elsewhere?"

Saddam Hussein, it seemed, was getting away with it. Then, after Secretary Cheney's flying visit to Saudi Arabia, everything changed. On Friday, August 10, President Mubarak finally succeeded in convening an emergency meeting of the Arab League in Cairo. The meeting became a near-brawl. At first the Iraqis refused to come. Then they objected to the presence of Kuwait's Emir, who, they said, no longer represented a country. During the lunch break a member of the Iraqi delegation threw a plate at the Kuwaitis. At one point the crown prince, Sheik Saad, fainted and had to be attended to by a doctor. The distraught Emir departed early. Tariq Aziz, the cigar-puffing Iraqi foreign minister who was to become so well known later in the crisis, announced calmly that the invasion was irreversible: "The Arabs will recognize eventually that this is historic fact and it was the right thing to do."

Iraq, however, had misjudged Hosni Mubarak. Although Egypt's president is a former air-force pilot, he has a reputation for mildness, bordering on docility. In the decade since taking office he has worked patiently to bring Egypt back into the Arab fold, from which it was expelled when Anwar Sadat made peace with Israel. Forming good relations with Iraq had been a central part of this policy of rehabilitation. But if the Iraqis expected Mubarak to accept the invasion of Kuwait meekly, they reckoned without the Arab sense of honor. It was, after all, President Mubarak who had assured the world, and the Americans, that Saddam Hussein would not invade Kuwait. He had said so because he had received a personal promise to that effect from Saddam Hussein himself. Now he felt personally betrayed.

Prodded by Mubarak, the Arab League broke with tradition and abandoned its rule that all decisions had to be unanimous. Twelve of the twenty governments represented voted in favor of a fierce resolution demanding Iraq's immediate withdrawal from Kuwait and the restoration of the legitimate government. More astonishingly still, the resolution called on member states to provide military forces to defend Saudi Arabia and the other Gulf states "against any outside reaction." Only three of the League's members—Iraq, Libya, and the PLO—voted against the resolution. Algeria and Yemen abstained, while Jordan, Sudan, and Mauritania expressed reservations. Later, it became clear that Egyptian and Moroccan troops would indeed go to Saudi Arabia. Even Syria, Iraq's rival but no friend of the West, promised to provide troops.

If the news reaching Saddam Hussein from Cairo was bad enough, even worse things were happening at the United Nations headquarters in New York. There, too, American diplomacy was meeting with dramatic success. The Iraqi president had not tried to clear his invasion with the Soviet Union. He knew that Mikhail Gorbachev, eager to rescue his economy by improving relations with America and Western Europe, would not have supported it. He also knew, as he himself had reminded his fellow Arab presidents in Amman six months earlier, that Soviet power in the world was waning. Yet he somehow failed to draw the proper conclusion, assuming from previous experience that there was still enough Soviet-American animosity at the United Nations to block a united stand against Iraq.

That illusion collapsed on the very day of the invasion, with Security Council Resolution 660. This condemned the Iraqi action and demanded an immediate, unconditional withdrawal. But it was only the beginning. Resolution 661, on August 6, imposed a complete trade ban, the only exceptions being for medicine and food "in humani-

tarian circumstances." Three days later Resolution 662 declared the annexation of Kuwait null and void. By the end of August two further resolutions had demanded the release of foreign nationals held in Iraq and called on member states cooperating with the exiled Kuwaiti government to stop and search all ships traveling to or leaving Iraq. The only dissenting voices on the Security Council were raised by the Cubans and Yemenis—temporary members without a Security Council veto. The Soviet Union, Iraq's nominal ally, with which Iraq still had a friendship treaty, gave all these resolutions its full support.

Saddam Hussein's errors were George Bush's gains. Even so, the mood that second weekend among the President's men in Kennebunkport was sober. The United States had confounded the world by its vigorous response to the challenge in Kuwait. But the confrontation was only just beginning, its end hard to discern. There was certainly no sign of Saddam Hussein taking fright at the American reaction. Having installed a puppet government on August 7, he annexed the country outright on August 8, proclaiming it Iraq's nineteenth province. For all Central Command's efforts, Iraq was reinforcing its garrison there faster than American troops were reaching Saudi Arabia. There was a real fear at the Pentagon that Iraq's tank divisions might strike across the border before the lightly armed American paratroopers could be reinforced with heavy armor. And even if that did not happen, another crisis was beginning to emerge. Saddam Hussein was taking hostages.

Oil-rich Gulf states tend to be full of foreigners. Workers from poor countries flood in to perform menial and manual tasks; consultants from rich ones arrive to oversee engineering and building projects. Iraq and Kuwait were no exception. The Iraqi invasion trapped about 3,000 U.S. citizens and the same number of Britons in Kuwait, with another 500 Americans and 2,000 Britons in Iraq itself. At least 200,000 workers from the Indian sub-continent were also stranded. Shortly after President Bush left for Maine, the Iraqis closed their borders, "for security reasons." Foreign diplomats would be allowed to come and go; other foreigners were trapped. Nobody official, at this stage, was uttering the word "hostage." The U.S. government, in particular, could hardly bear the thought that it was facing a replay, magnified, of the Iranian hostage crisis of 1979–81. All over the country, however, distraught relatives were once again tying yellow ribbons to their front doors and trees. In Kennebunkport and in Baghdad, the two presidents settled in for a siege. It was to continue for five turbulent months.

The Great Siege

Eyeball to eyeball—but the envoy for peace finds that it takes two to tango

Saddam Hussein, surveying his position in the middle of August, had few reasons for cheer. His invasion had left Iraq isolated at the bar of world opinion. The oil embargo had cut off his principal source of foreign cash. If he were running an ordinary country, the case for cutting his losses and pulling out of Kuwait would already have been overwhelming. But Iraq was not an ordinary country. It was a dictatorship whose people had been told for more than a decade that their dictator was infallible and all-powerful, a modern-day Nebuchadnezzar destined to rekindle the lost glories of Babylon. A Nebuchadnezzar does not slink off home just because the United Nations imposes some economic sanctions.

Besides, his position was not entirely without strengths. One was possession. For all the huffing and puffing from the United Nations, Kuwait was firmly under Iraq's control. With every passing day the Iraqi army strengthened its grip on the captured emirate. An American military rescue of Kuwait would not be feasible for many months. In the meantime, possession meant plunder. As the occupation continued, Iraqi soldiers stole 50,000 cars, stripped thousands of homes, carried off a vast horde of food, and seized millions of dollars in foreign currency and hundreds of millions in gold bars from the Kuwaiti central bank. Airplanes, lampposts, street-lights—even the contents of the Museum of Islamic Art—were eventually to find their way to Baghdad. All of this booty would help to soften the impact of the economic blockade, perhaps giving Saddam time to knock a hole in the siege wall Bush was building around him.

That wall had gone up with impressive speed, but the cement was not yet dry. Would the Arab world, despite what had happened in Cairo, really let a brother country be starved into submission by the supporters of Israel? How long would the new companionship between Gorbachev and Bush survive? And would Americans themselves have the stomach for a fight if thousands of their compatriots were trapped as "guests" inside Iraq? Saddam Hussein recalled America's experience in Vietnam. The superpower's inability to defeat a third-world foe had made a deep impression on him. He felt certain that as the costs and perils of a potential war mounted, pressure for compromise would begin to grow in Washington. In the end, he might have to retreat from part of Kuwait. But so long as he gained something—a slice of territory, say, or financial compensation—he could still march home a hero from his adventure.

In Washington, however, Bush was arriving at exactly the opposite conclusion. It was now clear that Saddam Hussein's ambitions were likely to capsize U.S. interests in the Gulf. As the confrontation developed, Bush's aims therefore evolved. Restoring Kuwait—the whole of Kuwait—was to become the minimum aim. But, to strengthen America's other allies in the area, it would also be desirable to make Hussein's withdrawal as humiliating as possible. Some influential voices in the administration went further still. They argued that Saddam Hussein should not only be evicted from Kuwait and humiliated. The region would not be safe until his over-mighty war machine, together with his chemical weapons and nuclear facilities, was destroyed as well.

To achieve any of these aims, whether by war or sanctions, President Bush's first priority had to be the establishment of a powerful armed force in Saudi Arabia. That process was likely to take many weeks, perhaps months. In the meantime, a three-part American strategy for winning in the Gulf would be developed.

First, the United States would keep its own profile in the conflict as low as possible. Actions against Saddam Hussein would be organized in the name of the United Nations and in close coordination with the Soviet Union. In addition, as many countries as possible had to be

bribed or cajoled into joining the U.S. and British forces in Saudi Arabia. If it came to war, the Americans would of course do the bulk of the fighting. But by making the force in Saudi Arabia as multinational as possible, and by bringing into it contingents from Muslim as well as Christian countries, Bush would be able to counter an Iraqi attempt to portray the conflict in terms of a Muslim "us" against a Western "them."

The strategy's second element was that the financial burden of defeating Saddam Hussein had to be spread widely. Only the United States had the ability to project a vast military force into the Arabian desert in order to reverse Iraqi aggression. But the Americans were not going to be the only or even the principal beneficiaries of the confrontation with Saddam Hussein. The United States imported 24 percent of its oil from the Gulf in 1989. Western Europe and Japan imported 42 percent and 67 percent respectively. Taken together, Japan and the members of the European Community enjoyed a gross domestic product of $8.8 trillion, compared to America's $5.4 trillion. Unless those countries could be made to accept their share of the responsibility, the price of defeating Saddam might be the crippling of the U.S. economy.

This worked. Saudi Arabia, having increased its oil production by some two million barrels a day to make up for the embargo on Iraqi and Kuwaiti oil, was earning large amounts of extra revenue, much of which went to pay for Desert Shield. The Kuwaiti government in exile dug deep into the revenues from its vast overseas assets to finance the recovery of its kingdom. Germany and Japan, unwilling politically and (arguably) unable constitutionally to take part in the military buildup, covered their embarrassment by making vast contributions. By the time

the air war was underway, the American budget director, Richard Darman, was able to report that America's allies had committed $51 billion to support the Gulf war.

The third element of Bush's strategy was to maintain the anti-Saddam solidarity of the Arab world. Any breaking of ranks by the Iranians or by Iraq's Arab neighbors would render the United Nations siege ineffective. But keeping the Arab world on the allied side was obviously going to be difficult. Although the Arab League had reacted fiercely to the Iraqi invasion, the vote had been split. And not all of the Arab governments that had voted against Iraq had the support of their own people. Unlike Britain and France, the United States had no colonial history in the Middle East. But that advantage had long ago been canceled out by its image as Israel's foremost armorer and protector. In any confrontation between the United States and Saddam Hussein, the instinct of millions of Arabs would be to support Saddam.

Hussein's first bold siege-breaking move came on August 12, in a televised "initiative." As expected, it was aimed at the Palestine issue, the most vulnerable point in American relations with the Arabs. The United States, the Iraqi leader said, had "lost its mind" when Iraq decided to "restore" its nineteenth province. By massing fleets and armies the Americans were in danger of starting a tragic war, on the pretext of opposing aggression. To unveil the falsity of this pretext, Iraq would therefore offer to reconsider its position in Kuwait if Israel pulled out, immediately and unconditionally, from the Arab territories it was occupying, and if Syria withdrew its occupying army from Lebanon. Thus was born the notion of "linkage," upon which so many false hopes of peace were to be built and then broken in the subsequent five-month countdown to war.

Although Saddam's move was cynical—he had been happy enough to forget about Palestine for most of the 1980s—it was also smart. It was received with rapture by Palestinians everywhere, even though the connection between the Israeli and Iraqi occupations was utterly false. Israel's conquest of the West Bank and Gaza in the war of 1967 had come about when the Jewish state was in genuine peril and launched a preemptive war against its neighbors. Iraq's invasion of Kuwait was an unprovoked grab for land. But these subtleties counted for little on the streets of the Arab world, where anti-Israeli passions, always strong, had been inflamed by Israel's harsh treatment of the Palestinians' three-year-old uprising against military occupation. In Arab eyes, the Americans' vigorous denunciation of Iraq's occupation of Kuwait was in glaring contrast with its toleration of the much older

Israeli occupation of the West Bank.

To shake off the charge of double standards, President Bush had to strike a delicate balance. His friendship with Israel was a threat to the Arab regimes supporting him against Iraq. To help these regimes, he needed both to distance himself from Israel, and to promise rapid progress on Palestine once Kuwait had been liberated. But tilting too far against Israel was also dangerous. It could antagonize Israel's supporters in Congress, where he would need support in any war against Iraq, and might also let Saddam Hussein score a propaganda victory by claiming credit for having reversed the American attitude to Palestine.

Miraculously, over the course of the following months, the administration managed to get the balance just about right. In October, when Israeli police shot dead nearly twenty Palestinians during a riot on Jerusalem's Temple Mount, Bush withdrew America's customary protection of the Israelis at the United Nations. The Israelis were angry, but their feelings were soothed when Yitzhak Shamir, the Israeli prime minister, visited Washington in December. Then, later that month, the Americans let it be known at the United Nations that they would, in principle, accept the idea of an international peace conference on the Palestine question, a long-standing Arab demand rejected by Mr. Shamir. But the conference, added the Americans, would have to be held "at the appropriate time." And the time was not yet ripe. This delicate balancing act was maintained. At no point did Bush accept Saddam Hussein's face-saving idea of "linkage"—even though some of his European allies were later tempted to do so.

As for Saddam Hussein, he waited only three days after launching his Palestine initiative before making a second bid to break the United Nations siege. On August 15, in a startling letter to President Rafsanjani, he offered to accept all the terms Iran had been laying down as the price of turning the two-year-old cease-fire between the two countries into a permanent peace. As a gesture of goodwill, he would pull out immediately from all the Iranian territory still under Iraqi control and release all Iranian prisoners of war. And, astonishingly, he would reinstate the 1975 border agreement between the two countries. In 1980, on television, Saddam Hussein had ripped up a copy of this agreement, which gave Iran and Iraq shared control of the strategic Shatt al-Arab waterway serving the Iraqi port of Basra. Grabbing control of the Shatt had been one of Saddam Hussein's main aims in invading Iran in 1980. Now he was throwing away the only gain Iraq had won in an eight-year war that had cost the participants nearly a million casualties.

President Rafsanjani, a famous opportunist, graciously accepted the offer. But if Saddam expected the concessions to buy him out of his siege, he was to be disappointed. The Iranians continued to denounce his invasion of Kuwait. Despite constant rumors, and the efforts of free-lance smugglers, no significant sanctions-busting took place across the Iran-Iraq border. Peace with Iran did at least enable Hussein to move several divisions from the Iranian border to "the great dueling arena" in Kuwait. But by throwing away his one gain from the Gulf war, he was running a huge risk at home. Several months later, he admitted as much. "You understand that after renouncing all my results after eight years of war with Iran, the Iraqi people would not forgive an unconditional retreat from Kuwait," he told Yevgeny Primakov, during one of the Soviet envoy's several visits to Baghdad. "And what would become of our access to the sea? It would be suicidal for me."

By comparison with these desperate maneuvers, the main elements of President Bush's strategy fell into place with a smoothness that only superpowerdom can confer. From time to time, attempts to work through the United Nations and keep the Soviet Union supportive looked shaky. In August, Soviet diplomats suggested reviving a moribund United Nations committee, the Security Council Military Staff Committee, which might in theory take operational command of the warships enforcing the blockade of Iraq. The idea of putting their fleets under the U.N.'s cumbersome command thoroughly alarmed the British and the Americans. But, by September, it was plain that President Gorbachev was sufficiently preoccupied by economic worries at home to give Bush a virtually free hand in Kuwait. At a meeting in Helsinki the two presidents issued a communiqué promising "additional steps" under the United Nations Charter if peaceful measures failed to end the Iraqi occupation.

The American plan to widen the military coalition assembling in Saudi Arabia was also a spectacular success. The British, with Mrs. Thatcher as prime minister, had come in from the start with naval and air forces. Later, in stages, they added substantial ground forces. The British 1st Armored Division, which included the "Desert Rats" who had defeated Rommel in the Second World War, was later to play a vital part in the battle for Kuwait. France's President Mitterrand, cooler about the idea of working jointly with the Americans in diplomacy, nevertheless sent forces to Saudi Arabia. Much later, the French Daguet Division found itself playing a daring role in the land battle deep inside Iraq. No other European country sent substantial numbers of ground troops, but warships and other forms of military help came from Australia, Argentina, Belgium, Canada, Denmark, Greece, Italy, Holland, Spain, and many other countries.

Bush's biggest coup, however, was to persuade two Arab countries—Egypt and Syria—to contribute more than 45,000 men between them to the military buildup. Egypt eventually sent two experienced armored divisions plus a commando regiment. Syria, whose staunchly anti-Israeli President Assad could never be accused of being an American stooge, sent an armored division. More than a thousand soldiers were also sent to Saudi Arabia by Morocco's pro-American King Hassan (a move he was to regret when Moroccan opinion swung violently behind Saddam Hussein once the war had started). Along with Saudi Arabia, the surviving members of the Gulf Cooperation Council—Oman, Qatar, Bahrain, and the United Arab Emirates—put armed forces and military bases at the alliance's disposal. At Saudi Arabia's request other Muslim troops arrived from Pakistan and Bangladesh.

By the beginning of November, Iraq had been under siege for three months, and the three legs of American strategy were firmly in place. A grand international military alliance was forming in and around the Arabian peninsula, with the full authority of the United Nations. Offers of money to pay for Desert Shield, and to compensate friendly countries hurt by the sanctions against Iraq, were pouring in from all sides. Saddam Hussein's efforts to make peace with Iran, and to use the Palestine question to split off the Arab wing of the coalition, had not broken the siege wall. All this was satisfying. Yet an uneasy mood prevailed among President Bush's inner circle.

The reason was simple: For all the pressure on him, Saddam Hussein was showing no sign whatsoever of relaxing his grip on Kuwait. Iraq's sea routes through the Gulf and the Jordanian port of Aqaba were being pinched off by allied warships. Inside Iraq many basic foodstuffs were now rationed, and the prices of others had soared. Thanks to the oil embargo, Iraq's dwindling hoard of foreign currency could not be replaced by new oil revenues. If sanctions could be kept in place for long enough, the Iraqi economy would certainly be ruined. But would even the ruination of his economy shake the Iraqi dictator's grip on Kuwait? A dictator, after all, dictates. Ordinary people might feel crushed by the burden of poverty, but Saddam Hussein had long ago extinguished all possibility of opposition or complaint. To judge by his bloodcurdling speeches, he would be quite willing to see his people slip into starvation before submitting to the hated "imperialists."

Besides, nobody in Washington could be sure by November how much longer the sanctions could be kept in place. Although Saddam Hussein's initial efforts to split off the Arab members of the alliance had failed, he was still trying. Most Arab regimes, shocked by the invasion of one Arab country by another, had decided to oppose him. Now he was appealing over the heads of the kings and presidents directly to the people. Here and there, since most Arab governments are unelected and unpopular, he struck a responsive chord. In Jordan, where a majority of the people are Palestinians, he had become an avenging hero, the new Saladin who would defeat the Americans and drive the Jews out of Palestine. Egyptians were less enamored. Many Egyptians had been migrant workers in Iraq, and had been wretchedly treated. Still, the thought of American servicemen (and women) defending the holy places of Islam made Egypt's Islamic opposition movement uncomfortable. Some newspapers had begun to talk about the "new crusaders" in the Saudi desert. Even in Syria, which usually smothers dissent as efficiently as Iraq, there was grumbling about President Assad's decision to take the side of the West and the over-rich Saudis against a radical Arab brother. America's Arab alliance was holding; but it would not necessarily last forever.

Although the non-Arab members of the alliance were more solid, each also had its own ideas about how the confrontation should end. On September 24, President Mitterrand had given a speech at the United Nations. In it he spoke of the need for Iraq to withdraw from Kuwait, but also dangled hope of a compromise. Mitterrand hinted that a satisfactory outcome would not have to include the return of the al-Sabah family to the Kuwaiti throne; instead, a referendum might be held to let Kuwaitis choose a new government. He also spoke at length of the need for an international conference on the problems of the whole region, implying some sympathy for Saddam's talk about linkage between Kuwait and Palestine. This alarmed the Americans, raising the specter of Saddam being able to give up Kuwait without suffering the humiliation the Americans now regarded as essential.

As for the Soviet Union, nothing was predictable. In Helsinki in September, Bush believed he had received

Gorbachev's agreement that, although it should be a last resort, military force might be necessary in order to push Saddam Hussein out of Iraq. Shortly afterward the Soviet foreign minister, Eduard Shevardnadze, warned the U.N. General Assembly that war might start "at any moment." In late October, however, Gorbachev sent out an abruptly different signal. His itinerant envoy, Yevgeny Primakov, had just paid one of his periodic visits to Baghdad, claiming to bring back "some signs"—with no details offered—of Iraqi flexibility. Now Gorbachev was apparently ruling out the use of force altogether. Even the Saudis were beginning to sound conciliatory, hinting that Kuwait's government in exile might consider territorial concessions in exchange for an Iraqi withdrawal. In Washington it was decided to send Secretary of State James Baker on an alliance-stiffening tour to Europe and the Middle East.

Baker set off on November 4. His mission, he said, was to ask America's friends "under what conditions, and subject to what circumstances, they would be willing to consider certain types of action." He was, in other words, going to find out which of the allies would if necessary be willing to fight to liberate Kuwait. In some ways the visit went well. In Riyadh, Baker was able to hammer out an agreement between General Schwarzkopf and the Saudis for a workable chain of military command if it came to war. At the Saudi mountain resort of Taif, Kuwait's exiled Emir told Baker that he wanted his country liberated "today, not tomorrow." In Cairo President Mubarak said he remained a staunch member of the alliance. In Ankara President Ozal is believed to have given his permission for America to use Turkish air bases in the event of fighting. And in Moscow Secretary of State Baker was told that Gorbachev's remark in Paris, appearing to rule out war under any circumstances, had been misinterpreted.

Even so, the Baker tour exposed a problem. Wherever he went, the secretary of state was told that any plan to use force against Iraq should first receive the explicit approval of the United Nations. This view was at odds with the formal position of the Americans and British. Since August, they had claimed that Article 51 of the United Nations Charter already gave the alliance a perfect right to go to war. This article says that a member state has the right to ask others for help in resisting aggression. Kuwait was a victim of aggression, and had asked its friends to reverse it. But it was becoming clear that a lot of foreign governments, and much domestic opinion, refused to swallow this line of argument. If Bush decided on war, and wanted to keep the world behind him, he would have to go back to the Security Council.

Doing so would be risky. What if the Security Council turned down an Anglo-American request for permission to fight? The Iraqis had been working tirelessly to drive a wedge between the British and Americans and the council's other three veto-wielding members, France, China, and the Soviet Union. Baker, however, thought the differences could be bridged. He had spent ninety minutes at Cairo airport talking to China's foreign minister, Qian Qichen. It seemed that although the Chinese were not keen on seeing military action, they would not necessarily use their veto. And Gorbachev was apparently standing by his Helsinki statement that "additional steps" against Iraq might be needed if sanctions failed. By the time the secretary of state reported back to Washington after his eight days of travel, the chances of pushing a war resolution through the Security Council were looking distinctly brighter.

At about the same time, once November's congressional elections were safely out of the way, Bush announced what was later recognized as the biggest military step since sending troops to Saudi Arabia back in August. The United States had already positioned a massive force of about 230,000 men and women and more than 800 battle tanks in the Gulf. Together with the hundreds of land and carrier-based allied aircraft in the region, this garrison was certainly powerful enough to deter an Iraqi onslaught on Saudi Arabia. The "strictly defensive" mission of Desert Shield had been achieved. Now Bush decided to add huge reinforcements, to ensure that the alliance had "an adequate offensive military option should that be necessary to achieve our common goals." The scale of the new effort was kept vague to begin with. But it soon emerged that another 200,000 or so personnel and another 1,000 tanks were to be shipped to the desert. The new forces would include two armored divisions and an armored cavalry regiment of the American VII Army Corps, based in Germany.

This was the army that was to have defended Europe from the Soviets. Moving it to Saudi Arabia to confront Saddam Hussein was the clearest signal yet that Bush's threat to use force if sanctions failed was no bluff. Iraq's representative at the United Nations accused the Americans of "blowing the horns of war," and tried without success to organize a Security Council debate about the reinforcements. But it was not only Iraq that was alarmed; many Americans were also taken aback. Until November, Congress had been content to support the President's moves in the crisis. Now there were stirrings of dissent. A powerful Democrat, Georgia's Senator Sam Nunn, argued that enlarging the garrison in the desert was a mistake. It would be costlier to sustain and so make it harder for the United States to wait for sanctions to work. Other congressmen started to ask when, or indeed whether, Congress could express an opinion on going to war.

Few people in America or Europe questioned the desirability of ending the Iraqi occupation of Kuwait. The debate was about means. Estimates leaked from the Pentagon suggested that the number of American dead in a war might run into tens of thousands, even if Saddam Hussein did not use his arsenal of deadly chemicals and poisonous gases. For many Americans, no likely gain in the Gulf seemed proportional to the price. Far better, they argued, to sit the crisis out until sanctions did the trick, even settle for something less than an unconditional Iraqi withdrawal. A procession of former heads of state made free-lance visits to Iraq, adding to the appetite for compromise. All came home bearing a handful of freed hostages, as well as hints of Iraqi flexibility.

At the end of November, an undaunted President Bush set off on a week of travels, taking in talks with Mikhail Gorbachev and other world leaders in Paris, a Thanksgiving Day visit to the troops in Saudi Arabia, and meetings with President Mubarak of Egypt and President Assad of Syria. He returned home confident that the Security Council would now be ready to pass a resolution authorizing war. On November 29 it did so. Resolution 678, the twelfth resolution passed against Iraq since the invasion of Kuwait, for the first time set a deadline for Iraq's withdrawal. If Iraqi troops were not out by January 15, member states would have permission to use "all necessary means" to liberate Kuwait. The vote was followed on the next day by a surprise. In the interests of going "the extra mile" for peace, said President Bush, he was willing to receive the Iraqi foreign minister in Washington, and to send James Baker to Baghdad to see Saddam Hussein. The point would not be negotiation—there could be no compromising on the demand for a complete and unconditional Iraqi withdrawal—but to make sure through an eye-to-eye encounter that the Iraqi dictator understood America's resolve.

Eyeballing Saddam Hussein was not, of course, the only purpose of the President's initiative. Despite his success at the Security Council, Bush had not yet persuaded Congress to support military action in the Gulf. Baker's mission to Baghdad might frighten Hussein into retreating. If it did not, the attempt would at least silence domestic critics who had complained that the administration refused to talk directly to Baghdad. Either way, Bush would be a winner. But the initiative also entailed a risk. It was all very well for the U.S. to say that there would be no bargaining in Baghdad. What, though, if Iraq's president used Baker's visit to announce some unilateral concession, such as a withdrawal from every part of Kuwait except the Rumaila oil field and the coveted offshore islands? Baker would undoubtedly retort that a partial withdrawal was not good enough. But under those circumstances the chances of Congress supporting war for the sake of some forlorn mud flats athwart the Shatt al-Arab waterway were remote.

Thanks to a quibble over dates, there was to be no meeting between James Baker and Saddam Hussein in Baghdad. Yet Bush's initiative may have brought an unintended dividend. On December 6, while the Americans and Iraqis were still arguing about the date of the meeting, Hussein abruptly announced that the 3,000 Western hostages held as "guests" in Iraq were free to go, "with our apologies for all harm and forgiveness from God almighty." The reason for his decision is obscure. Just possibly, the Iraqi president thought or was tricked into thinking that the Americans were at last on the brink of making the war-averting compromise he had been hoping for. Many Western commentators had, after all, seen the Baker mission as the prelude to America backing down. The United States was also hinting at the United Nations that, while still rejecting "linkage," it was becoming more interested in an international conference on Palestine. Whatever the reason, virtually all the hostages had jubilantly left Iraq by the middle of December.

The last few weeks were an emotional roller coaster. First it looked as if the Iraqi-American talks would never happen. Then, when the European Community threatened to step into the diplomatic vacuum, Bush offered to let James Baker meet Tariq Aziz in Geneva. As before, the President made it plain that this would be a chance to read the riot act to the Iraqis, nothing more. There would be "no negotiations, no compromises, no attempts at face-saving, and no rewards for aggression." By now Bush could afford to talk loudly. He was carrying a big stick. The allied military buildup was nearly complete and the United Nations had given him the equivalent of a blank check for war. And yet, somehow, the message did not get through to Baghdad. The first thing Tariq Aziz did on arriving in Geneva was to make it plain that Iraq was still insisting on linkage between Kuwait and Palestine. "If there is a genuine, sincere intention to make peace in the whole region of the Middle East we are ready to reciprocate," he said. "But if we are to hear the same kind of talk we have heard over the last few months, we are going to have the proper answer."

On January 9, Baker and Aziz talked to each other for six barren hours across a narrow table in Geneva. It was a dialogue of the deaf. The U.S. team tried to convey to the Iraqis the impossibility of their position, the nearness of the deadline, the superiority of allied military power, the inevitability of Iraq's defeat in any clash of arms. Baker delivered a personal letter from Bush warning Hussein against making yet another "miscalculation." But Aziz was carrying no mandate from Baghdad to bend the knee. Instead he whiled away the hours with a rendering of Iraq's growing litany of complaints. As for Bush's letter, it was left lying on the table. It was, said Aziz afterwards, too impolite to take back to Hussein in Baghdad.

Few people had expected peace to break out in Geneva. The U.S. had made it abundantly clear that nothing less than a complete and humiliating Iraqi reversal would remove the threat of war. But the abjectness of the failure was nevertheless a surprise. Geneva gave Hussein a golden chance to offer something: a partial with-drawal, a clearer offer to pull out of Kuwait in return for progress on Palestine, perhaps a retraction of his claim to have annexed Kuwait for all time. Any one of these things could have split the anti-Iraqi alliance, or made it harder for Bush to win the support of Congress for military action. And yet there was nothing. In a press conference Tariq Aziz did not even utter the word "Kuwait." He did not say firmly that Iraq would give up its nineteenth province if Israel left the West Bank. Asked whether Iraq would attack Israel in the event of a war with the alliance, he said simply, "Of course." His obstinacy was a gift to the White House. Three days later, after much tense debate, both the Senate (in a close vote) and the House of Representatives granted Bush authority to wage war against Iraq and expel its armed forces from Kuwait.

Just why Saddam Hussein squandered the opportunity at Geneva remains a mystery. He may by then already have been reconciled to war. He may still have thought the Americans were bluffing. But it is also possible that he misunderstood the signals he was getting from France. Before the Baker-Aziz meeting, the Americans were doing everything possible to impress on Iraq that this was the last slender hope of avoiding a war. On the very day that Baker and Aziz were talking in Geneva, however, President Mitterrand gave a press conference in Paris. To Washington's relief, the French president said that France insisted on Iraq observing the deadline set out by the United Nations. But he also reserved France's right to make another peace bid if the Geneva talks failed. France had always been warmer than the British and Americans to the idea of linkage. Perhaps the Iraqi leader concluded that if he said no to the Americans in Geneva he would still have time to say yes to a better French offer later on.

If so, he never got the better offer. France did try, in the dying days before January 15, to talk the Security Council into issuing a call for an international conference to discuss "all" the problems of the region. The effort was brushed irritably aside by the U.S. and the British. Meanwhile it fell not to France but to Javier Perez de Cuellar, the United Nations secretary-general, to make an eleventh-hour visit to Iraq in the hope of changing Hussein's mind. The Peruvian diplomat saw Hussein on January 13, two days before the deadline, and after being kept waiting for several hours. When he was at last granted an audience, his attempts to talk Saddam into considering a with-drawal were rebuffed. Perez de Cuellar returned to New York in a despondent mood. "You need two for tango," he told reporters. "I wanted to dance but I didn't find any nice lady for dancing with."

For nearly five months, from August 2 until January 15,

the world had held its breath as George Bush and Saddam Hussein sat out their bitter siege. The U.S. president had decided at the outset that there would be no compromise, that Hussein would be forced one way or another to skulk out of Kuwait with his tail between his legs. The Iraqi president, for his part, had refused to be cowed. In the last days of peace, he gave a defiant speech to a group of Islamic clerics, summoned to Baghdad from around the world. Dressed in full military regalia, he told them that Iraq would triumph in the forthcoming war. He wished, he said, that he could show his visitors the military preparations that had been made in Kuwait. There they would see no Iraqi tanks and few vehicles, because they had been hidden underground in shelters. When the Americans attacked, the tanks and soldiers would emerge to destroy them. In the air, he said, Iraq's enemies planned to jam radio communication between pilots. But Iraqi pilots had trained to complete their missions without receiving radio instructions. Iraq, he said, had learned about war in eight years of fighting Iran in the desert, "unlike the Americans, using military manuals."

The speech impressed the Islamic faithful. They clapped and cheered. Some kissed the dictator's hand, tears running down their cheeks. The emotional scenes were broadcast on television, and watched later by the allies' military planners in the Saudi desert. They, too, were happy at what they heard and saw. Saddam Hussein had shown once again that he knew how to chill the blood. He had also shown that he understood nothing at all about modern war.

Orders for Battle

The coalition commanders think Hussein has misunderstood a thing or two

Armies, it is said, never learn from victories, only defeats. The two armies squaring up against one another in the Arabian desert in the summer and fall of 1990 were both preoccupied by the memory of earlier wars. The Iraqi army had come out well from its bloody war against Iran. With victory fresh in its mind, it made the fatal mistake of believing that it could beat the United States by applying the same strategy that had succeeded so well against its third-world neighbor. The American army, in contrast, had not fought a major war since the failure in Vietnam. Most of its top commanders, not only Generals Powell and Schwarzkopf, were Vietnam veterans who had spent more than a decade analyzing the lessons of Vietnam. They went into the Kuwaiti enterprise determined that the United States would never repeat that war's mistakes.

The starting point of any strategic plan is the enemy. For Central Command, instructed to prepare a plan to drive Iraq out of Kuwait, the most surprising thing about the Iraqi armed forces was their sheer size. Iraq was a poor country, yet it was capable of keeping nearly a million men under arms. This, moreover, was not an infantry army but an army organized around a lavishly equipped armored force. The Iraqi fleet of some 5,000 tanks was one of the biggest in the world. More than 1,000 of these were modern T-72s with a powerful 125mm gun—not the most modern tanks the Soviet Union could provide, but good nonetheless. In war the tanks would be supported by about 6,000 armored personnel carriers and some 5,000 artillery pieces, including Soviet-made multiple rocket launchers and South Africa's excellent G5 howitzer, with a range of twenty-four miles. Iraq was also, by third-world standards, a big operator of modern attack helicopters, with about 160 French and Soviet machines.

Iraq's air force was less impressive. It possessed more than 600 combat aircraft, but only a fraction—MiG-25 and MiG-29 fighters, Su-24 and Su-25 bombers—belonged to the latest generation of machines. The Iraqi air force, moreover, had given a lackluster performance in the Iran-Iraq war. Despite outnumbering the Iranians, its pilots tended to avoid air-to-air combat and to drop their bombs inaccurately from great altitudes. From the outset, General Schwarzkopf knew that if this mediocre force chose to fight it would be quickly chopped out of the skies by the vast land and carrier-based air armada the United States and its allies were assembling in the Gulf. In a war, the allies could count on air superiority. The unknown question was how useful that would be.

Since the Six-Day War of 1967, when Israel destroyed four Arab air forces on the ground in a single day, Arab leaders have been obsessed about the danger of air attack. Saddam Hussein, who in 1981 saw his Osirak nuclear reactor near Baghdad knocked out by a daring Israeli air raid, was no exception. He had responded in three ways. First, Iraq made a huge investment in air defenses, so that the army could continue to function even if it lost control of the air. In the Arab-Israeli war of 1973 Hussein had been impressed by the large number of Israeli aircraft shot down by Egypt's and Syria's Soviet-made surface-to-air missiles and guns. The airplane, he concluded, was no longer king of the desert battlefield. Iraq's armored divisions were equipped with Soviet or French tracked surface-to-air missile launchers, plus rapid-firing guns designed to chew up aircraft that tried to avoid the missiles by attacking at low levels.

His second precaution was to build a large number of hardened aircraft shelters, well concealed and protected by blast walls, to prevent the air force from being knocked out on the ground in another 1967-style attack. Hunkering down under concrete is no formula for winning a war in the air, but it is at least a means of preserving some of your aerial capacity in the face of attack by a superior enemy. Iraqi airfields were also huge—several times as big as Warsaw Pact airfields in East Germany—so that putting their runways out of action would be immensely difficult. In principle, Iraqi aircraft that weathered the American attacks in their shelters should be able to venture out from time to time for hit-and-run raids against enemy ground forces.

Saddam Hussein's third step was to compensate for weakness in the air by finding alternative ways to carry the battle to his enemy's rear. The answer, used to considerable effect in the Iran-Iraq war, was the medium-range ballistic missile. The inaccurate Scuds that the Soviet Union had sold to Iraq deliver a warhead of about half a ton of high explosive, a small fraction of the payload that could be delivered by a fighter-bomber. But ballistic mis-

siles re-enter the atmosphere too fast to be intercepted by fighter aircraft or most types of antiaircraft missile. Possession of the Scuds, some of which the Iraqis had modified to extend their range beyond the usual 300 miles, gave Hussein a reliable way to hit at his enemies' capital cities even if his air force was not up to the job. During the Iran-Iraq war the Iraqis had lobbed missiles into Tehran, the Iranian capital, sowing panic and leading to the evacuation of much of the city.

After that war, Hussein also accelerated attempts to add another powerful element to his arsenal: unconventional weapons. In 1988 the extensive use of poison gas helped Iraq win the final battles against Iran. At the end of the war, Saddam Hussein ordered their use against his own dissident Kurds, killing 5,000 men, women, and children in a single attack on the town of Halabja. Perfecting these weapons, and the means of delivering them, became a priority during the postwar period. Two large production centers were built at Samarra, northwest of Baghdad, and at Al-Fallujah, west of Baghdad. These facilities were believed to churn out mustard gas as well as the deadly nerve agents tabun and sarin. A chemical-weapons research center was established at Salman Pak, twenty-five miles southeast of the capital. In April 1990, Hussein announced that Iraq had made a breakthrough in this area, having become the first third-world country to produce the advanced "binary" chemical warheads owned by the superpowers.

Saddam Hussein never boasted about any efforts to acquire a nuclear bomb. Indeed, he vehemently denied trying. Iraq had signed the Nuclear Nonproliferation Treaty and put its known nuclear facilities under the safeguards of the International Atomic Energy Agency. Even

the war began was how well, and how intelligently, the Iraqis would actually fight. To work that out, General Schwarzkopf's command began an intensive reappraisal of Iraq's performance in the war against Iran. From that appraisal the detailed plan for Desert Storm, the operation to liberate Kuwait, began to emerge.

Iraq had more or less won the war against Iran. Yet the war was not the triumph Iraqi propaganda later portrayed it to be. Iraq's initial invasion of Iran in 1980 was poorly conducted, and became bogged down after the first few months of fighting. Thereafter its army settled into a defensive pattern. Iraqi military engineers dug vast earthworks and trench systems. Interlocking road networks were constructed behind the front lines so that tanks and artillery could be moved quickly from sector to sector to respond to any Iranian initiatives. For most of the eight years of the war, it was Iran that had done all the attacking on the ground, even though the Iranians were desperately short of modern equipment and spare parts. When Iran's ferocious but poorly armed Revolutionary Guards launched their assaults, the Iraqis broke up their formations by employing massive artillery barrages.

The Iraqi strategy was unimaginative, but it worked. In February 1984 the Iranians launched a quarter of a million men in a "final offensive." It was repelled, with heavy losses. The same thing happened a year later. In 1986 the Iranians had better luck. They succeeded in crossing the Shatt al-Arab waterway, capturing the Fao peninsula, and threatening the port of Basra, Iraq's second city. But Basra never fell, and Iran's repeated attempts to take it wasted tens of thousands of its soldiers' lives. In 1987–88, in a first sign that its army was running out of steam, Iran failed to mount its usual winter push. Then came a string of Iranian retreats: first from the Fao peninsula in April 1988 and later from most of the remaining bits of territory Iranian troops had captured on the Iraqi side of the border. In the end, the Iranians simply wore themselves out in their doomed attacks on Iraq's defenses. By July 1988 they were suing for peace. The Iran-Iraq war was won, First-World-War style, by attrition rather than maneuver.

This experience made a profound impression on both Saddam Hussein and his senior command. They interpreted the decision of an exhausted Iran to give up the fight as a token of their own brilliant generalship. The truth, that after eight years of war the much poorer Iranians had virtually nothing left to fight with, was conveniently brushed aside. As a result, the shopworn tactics of the Iran-Iraq war were to be spruced up and tried again in Kuwait. The Iraqi army would hunker down in deep fortifications, and inflict huge losses on the allies when they

so, few experts in the West doubted that the Iraqis were working covertly as hard as possible to get a bomb. The most recent evidence was Iraq's attempt in 1990 to smuggle high-quality electrical capacitors, which can be used in nuclear triggers, through London's Heathrow airport. Some intelligence services reported that Iraq was building gas centrifuges with which to enrich uranium. Others worried that Iraq had salvaged enough fissile material from its bombed Osirak reactor to put together a crude atomic device that could be used against American forces in Saudi Arabia. On his Thanksgiving Day visit to the desert, President Bush said those who assumed an Iraqi bomb was years away might have underestimated the threat. If there was to be a war, the destruction of Iraq's nuclear and chemical weapons programs was clearly going to be one of its aims.

A powerful and experienced land army, a smallish air force, plenty of antiaircraft artillery, medium-range ballistic missiles and a proven chemical-weapons capability. This was the war machine General Schwarzkopf knew he would be up against if the President gave the order to turn Desert Shield into an operation to recapture Kuwait by force. On paper, it added up to a formidable task. What nobody in Central Command could be sure about until tried to storm the defense line. After all, as Saddam Hussein had told April Glaspie, America was not a society that could accept heavy losses in battle. He, in contrast, had thrown away hundreds of thousands of Iraqi lives in his previous war, then bragged about it afterward. He might not defeat the Americans, but he could surely inflict enough pain to prevent them from scoring too lopsided a victory in Kuwait. Fighting a superpower to a standstill, or falling back inside Iraq after putting up strong resistance, could be portrayed later as a victory in the Arab and Muslim worlds.

How could Desert Storm be crafted to counter this strategy? One guiding principle, clear from the outset, was that the United States would employ massive and overwhelming force. In Vietnam, the army had been committed in dribs and drabs to a fight that dragged on for nearly ten inconclusive years. This time, General Powell had asked the President not to join battle until he had a big enough force in the desert to make the war brief and one-sided. This meant fending off impatient allies. Israel, accustomed after its many wars to fighting with too few forces and inadequate preparation, urged the Americans to attack early. Delay, it warned, would give the Iraqi army too much time to dig in, and give Saddam Hussein too much political wriggle-room. The Arab allies were equally anxious. Saudi Arabia and Egypt, calling in public for sanctions to be given time, were privately urging Bush to act. They feared instability at home if the crisis were prolonged. The Americans brushed off these demands, waiting until General Schwarzkopf had a mighty force in Saudi Arabia before launching the land war.

The reinforcement operations came in two stages: the first designed to build a credible defense and the second to build a force big enough to go on the attack. The choice of units and the timing of their arrival was dictated by practical necessities. During the defensive buildup, Central Command's officers sent whichever forces were most readily available: ships that were nearby and troops that were in the highest states of readiness and the easiest to move, the airborne units. However, from the outset, they were planning continuously for a large buildup, including substantial numbers of heavy armored units. Normal military foresight dictated that warning orders went out to a number of heavy units early in the fall, well before any

decision was taken to ship them to the desert. Even if a decision had been taken in August to send all the American units that were eventually sent, it would have been impossible to funnel them in much earlier than they actually did arrive.

Thus once the tap was turned on in August, the reinforcement operation proceeded more or less continuously. As additional forces were sent, plans were being constantly redrawn to encompass even more. By the beginning of November the American and allied forces available in Saudi Arabia constituted a substantial force: if not the beginnings of an offensive force, at least a solid defensive one. If the Iraqis had invaded Saudi Arabia in August, they might well have got to the oil fields or, worse still, into the ports of Jubail and Dammam (without which the subsequent American buildup would have been well-nigh impossible) before air strikes and harassment attacks by the two airborne divisions could have stopped their advance across the open desert and along the one coastal road. Once the American marine division, the 24th Infantry Division and the British armored division were in place, Saudi Arabia was probably defendable near the border.

Throughout November, however, the reinforcement operations went on at full steam, supposedly still building a defensive force, but in reality building an offensive one. After Secretary of Defense Cheney's announcement in late November that another 200,000 men were going to the Gulf (to add to the 230,000 or so that were there then; the eventual total was nearly 540,000) there could no longer be any doubt that an offensive was in the cards. Shortly afterward Britain announced it was sending a second armored brigade, the other half of its 1st Armored

Allied Forces in the Gulf Theater

AFGHANISTAN	300 *mujahedin* troops
ARGENTINA	1 destroyer, 1 corvette, 2 air force transport planes
AUSTRALIA	1 guided-missile destroyer, 1 frigate, 1 supply ship, 2 surgical teams
BAHRAIN	3,000 troops
BANGLADESH	6,000 troops
BELGIUM	1 frigate, 2 minesweepers, 2 landing ships, 1 supply ship, 6 C-130 transport planes
BRITAIN	43,000 troops, 6 destroyers, 4 frigates, 3 minesweepers, 5 support ships, 168 tanks, 300 armored vehicles, 70 Tornado and Jaguar combat jets
CANADA	2 destroyers, 1 supply ship, 12 C-130 transport planes, 24 CF-18 bombers
CZECHOSLOVAKIA	200 chemical-warfare specialists
DENMARK	1 corvette
EGYPT	40,000 troops, including 2 armored divisions and 5,000 Special Forces paratroopers
FRANCE	18,000 troops, 60 combat aircraft, 120 helicopters, 40 tanks, 100 armored vehicles, 1 missile cruiser, 3 destroyers, 4 frigates
GREECE	1 frigate
HONDURAS	150 troops
HUNGARY	40 medical personnel
ITALY	2 corvettes, 3 frigates, 1 supply ship, 4 minesweepers, 10 Tornado ground attack aircraft
JAPAN	medical personnel and supplies
KUWAIT	11,000 troops
MOROCCO	1,700 troops
THE NETHERLANDS	2 frigates, 1 supply ship
NEW ZEALAND	3 C-130 Hercules transport planes, 1 medical team
NIGER	500 troops
NORWAY	1 Coast Guard cutter, 1 transport ship
OMAN	25,500 troops, 63 airplanes, 4 Exocet-armed ships
PAKISTAN	7,000 troops
THE PHILIPPINES	medical personnel
POLAND	2 rescue ships
PORTUGAL	1 naval logistics ship
QATAR	1 squadron of Mirage F-1E fighter planes
ROMANIA	360 medical personnel, 180 chemical warfare experts
SAUDI ARABIA	118,000 troops, 550 tanks, 180 combat planes, 8 frigates
SENEGAL	500 troops
SIERRA LEONE	30 medical personnel
SINGAPORE	35-man medical team
SOUTH KOREA	5 C-130 Hercules transport planes, 150-man medical team
SPAIN	1 frigate, 2 corvettes, 1 supply ship, 1 C-130 transport plane
SWEDEN	field hospital and medical personnel
SYRIA	17,000 troops, 300 T-62 tanks
UNITED ARAB EMIRATES	40,000 troops, 80 combat planes, 15 ships, 200 tanks
UNITED STATES	540,000 troops, 6 aircraft carriers, nuclear submarines, 2,000 tanks, 2,200 armored personnel carriers, 1,700 helicopters, 100 warships, 1,800 airplanes

These figures are approximate. They have been compiled from various sources, including the Center for Defense Information, Reuters, The New York Times, and the U.S. Department of Defense.

Divison, plus a lot of extra aircraft, artillery, and medical support.

With an Anglo-American order of battle this strong, supplemented by the considerable Arab and other allied forces, the question for General Schwarzkopf was not whether he could drive the Iraqis out of Kuwait. That was a foregone conclusion. The issue was whether he could avoid being sucked into a battle of attrition.

One way to avoid heavy losses would be to ensure that the land war in Kuwait would, unlike the Iran-Iraq war, become a rapid war of armored movement, not a static war of artillery bombardments. When the land campaign started, the allies did just that, by dashing in a left hook through thinly defended parts of the Iraqi desert instead of banging their heads against the strong defense line the Iraqis had built inside Kuwait. Some way would also have to be found to defeat Iraq's Republican Guard, an elite strike force of eight armored and mechanized divisions which operated Saddam Hussein's best tanks and artillery. Here the Americans had high hopes that the appearance on a desert battlefield for the first time of swarms of modern attack helicopters would help tilt the armored battles their way.

Helicopters had been used against tanks before. Both Syrian and Israeli helicopters knocked out a number of each other's tanks during the Lebanon war of 1982. Iraq itself possessed forty or so Mi-24 "Hinds," a Soviet-built attack helicopter that saw extensive service in Afghanistan. But the helicopter force the Americans deployed in the Gulf was in a different league, both in quality and quantity. Although exact numbers are unavailable, this force may have included up to 350 Cobra and Apache helicopters. The Apache, the newer of the two, is a rugged and well-armored machine that can carry up to sixteen Hellfire laser-guided missiles as well as its rapid-fire armor-piercing cannon. Flying within a few feet of the ground, capable of speeds of nearly 200mph, and fitted with magnificent night-vision equipment, the Apache promised to revolutionize the armored battlefield.

The key to avoiding a war of attrition would, however, be the effective use of air power. Indeed, air supremacy promised not only to prevent allied forces from being sucked into attrition, but also to make attrition work in reverse: against Iraq and in favor of the alliance.

How? The British and American air commanders were confident that Saddam Hussein had misunderstood the lessons of the 1973 Arab-Israeli war. In that war, air-defense missiles had indeed put a dent in the wings of the famous Israeli air force. But to compare the position of the Israelis in 1973 with that of the Americans and their allies

nearly eighteen years later was ridiculous. In 1973 Israel had been taken by surprise and its army was in danger of being overrun on two fronts. Its small air force had to divide its attention between attacks on the enemy's missile systems and close support for the beleaguered ground troops.

The allies, in contrast, had moved into the Gulf with a huge air force, perhaps the most powerful ever assembled. The Americans alone had nearly 1,500 aircraft available; their British, French, Italian, and Arab allies several hundred more. An air fleet this size could attack Iraqi targets at leisure, and still keep aircraft in reserve to respond to emergencies at the front. If General Schwarzkopf's armies lurked out of Iraqi artillery range during this air phase, he could hurt Iraq more than Iraq with its relatively primitive Scud missiles could hurt him. To take the war to the Americans, the Iraqi army could of course venture out from the safety of its bunkers and launch an attack into Saudi Arabia. But then it would be indulging in an unfamiliar American-style war of movement, not the static bloodletting Saddam Hussein was counting on in order to break the allies' will to fight on.

If the Iraqi president had underestimated the sheer size of the allied air forces, he had also underestimated the impact of technology. After all, Israel's air force had recovered from the missile shock of 1973. In 1982, when Israel invaded Lebanon, its air force destroyed a dense array of Syrian surface-to-air missiles in Lebanon by using sophisticated electronic countermeasures and attacking the missiles' radar systems with antiradiation weapons. The Americans had taken this many steps further. Allied bombers going into attacks in the forthcoming war would often be accompanied by "Wild Weasels," Phantom jets stuffed with electronics and able to fire supersonic HARM antiradiation missiles back along the beam of any air-defense radar turned on in the course of the attack. Even more important, the Americans had the ability to attack the Iraqis with entire families of "stand-off" weapons: weapons that could be fired accurately at small targets from many miles away, without exposing the attackers to danger.

The most spectacular of these weapons was the navy's Tomahawk cruise missile, which had been designed originally to carry nuclear weapons. The nonnuclear version has a range of some 700 miles when fired from a warship (shorter than the nuclear version because the 1,000-pound warhead leaves less room for fuel). It flies low, navigating toward its target by comparing the readings from its altimeter with a terrain map compiled by satellite and stored in its computer memory. As it closes on the target, it switches to a second method of navigation. The image from a television camera mounted in its nose is compared with an image of the target stored in its computer in digital form. This way, in principle, it can guide itself toward, and through, a particular window in a building it has been sent to destroy from hundreds of miles away.

Another only slightly less spectacular missile was the navy's SLAM (Standoff Land Attack Missile), a version of the Harpoon antiship missile. The SLAM derivative has a range of around seventy miles, and finds its way to the target by reading signals from a fleet of navigational satellites, known as the Global Positioning System, with which the United States has girdled the earth. As it closes in, the SLAM turns on an infrared camera and transmits the picture to a controlling aircraft, which guides it the rest of the way. When war came, two such missiles were used by aircraft operating from a carrier in the Red Sea to attack an Iraqi power plant. The first blasted a hole in the

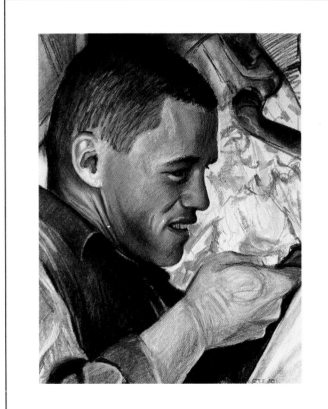

wall; the second steered through the hole to explode inside.

The standoff principle was incorporated in many other battlefield weapons, such as the Hellfire laser-guided missile that would enable Apache helicopters to knock out Iraqi tanks five miles away. In a sense, even the F-117 Stealth fighter is a standoff weapon. Designed to be invisible to radar, the Stealth would be able to fly into Iraq under cover of night and make pinpoint attacks on well-defended targets. These weapons worked in exercises. If they worked in real combat conditions, they might, like the English longbow at the battles of Crécy and Agincourt, make the "mother of all battles" a more lopsided affair than the enemy ever imagined.

Apart from making attrition work in reverse, the allied advantage in the air conferred two more advantages which General Schwarzkopf was eager to exploit. By starting the war with a lengthy air-only campaign, he would be able to pick off targets in Iraq first and then walk the war backward toward Kuwait. This was important if President Bush was to achieve all his aims. As far as the United Nations was concerned, it had given authority only for the liberation of Kuwait. But by the time the Americans had decided on war, their aims had expanded. In addition to freeing Kuwait, Bush wanted to draw the teeth of Saddam's war machine. That would not only mean destroying airfields, aircraft, and armor but also poison-gas factories and nuclear-research facilities. With luck, those facilities could be flattened from the air before the battle for Kuwait had even been joined.

Finally, if it was used intelligently, air supremacy would give the allies a political instrument against Saddam Hussein by bringing home to ordinary Iraqis the full extent of the disaster into which his policies had led them. During the Iran-Iraq war, the regime had managed to largely insulate Baghdad and the Iraqi hinterland from the carnage taking place at the front. An Iranian missile would occasionally land in the capital, but such events were rare. In this war the allies were determined to make the leadership pay an immediate, internal political penalty for its invasion of Kuwait. There was no question of carpet bombing Baghdad with B-52s. Western public opinion would not have accepted the intentional slaughter of innocent civilians. The answer, once again, would be to make full use of the new precision technology. Baghdad's people would not be deliberately attacked but their quality of life would be. How would Iraqis feel about their nineteenth province if the price of keeping it meant doing without telephones, light, electricity, and running water? The world would soon find out.

The Scud Shock

Israel looks again at its audacious secret plan for retaliation

At midnight, New York time, on January 15, the deadline for Iraq to withdraw from Kuwait under Resolution 678 expired. On the next day, a Wednesday, nothing happened. Then, as Wednesday slipped into Thursday in the Middle East, the blow fell. Out at sea in the darkness of the Gulf, American navy personnel pressed the buttons that would send a first salvo of fifty-two cruise missiles roaring off from the battleships *Wisconsin* and *Missouri* toward their designated targets in downtown Baghdad and other parts of Iraq. At the same time, hundreds of aircraft—fighters, bombers, jammers, and tankers—took off from carriers and from airfields all over the Arabian peninsula. Most of the aircraft were American, but British, Saudi, and Kuwait air forces also flew in this first strike. The war had begun.

Two hours later, President Bush addressed the nation. "As I report to you," he said, "air attacks are underway against military targets in Iraq. We are determined to knock out Saddam Hussein's nuclear bomb potential. We will also destroy his chemical-weapons facilities. Much of Saddam's artillery and tanks will be destroyed. Our operations are designed to best protect the lives of all the coalition forces by targeting Saddam's vast military arsenal. Initial reports from General Schwarzkopf are that our operations are proceeding according to plan." The President said he hoped that fighting would not go on for long and that casualties would be held to a minimum. He did not specify what a "long time" was—days, weeks, or months—or whether casualties would run into hundreds or thousands. From that night until the end of the war, the only thing the public could do was speculate.

By some accounts, the timing of the attack took Saddam Hussein by surprise. Newspapers had reported that the fresh troops America was bringing in from Germany would not be fully ready for battle until mid-February. But the case for starting the war right away was overwhelming. It would nip in the bud any further diplomatic attempts to let Iraq withdraw unpunished from Kuwait, while allowing a full three months for fighting before the desert became hot again and the Islamic holy month of Ramadan began. And it was always likely that the attack, when it came, would come at night. Many allied strike aircraft (the American F-111s, Stealth F-117s, A-6s, F-15Es; American and Canadian F-18s; and the British and Italian Tornados) carried specialized radars and infrared sensors to help them operate in darkness or bad weather. They would do well at night, whereas Iraqi air-defense artillery, much of which was aimed by eye, would be at its least effective.

The first wave of strikes on that first night went like clockwork. The attacking aircraft had been assigned to a large variety of targets, including Iraq's command-and-control centers, airfields, Scud missile sites, radar stations, and chemical-weapons storage depots. After three hours they had all returned safely to their bases. Virtually none of this aerial activity was visible to the outside world. The exception was in Baghdad, where a handful of Western journalists, including a team from America's Cable News Network, had elected to stay behind. From their room at the Al-Rashid hotel, the CNN reporters were able to record and describe the crackle of tracer bullets and the thump of bombs falling on the city. Baghdadis exploring town the next day found that key targets—the telecommunications center, the defense ministry, the Baath party headquarters, the presidential palace—had been demolished, leaving surrounding buildings eerily unscathed. It was, said one reporter, as if the allies had been practicing "microsurgery" on Baghdad.

The vivid accounts from the Iraqi capital, together with a series of upbeat briefings in Riyadh and Washington, created an atmosphere of near-euphoria on the first day of the war. The impression among many laymen was

that the battle was as good as over. Yet the apparently effortless pinpoint attacks on Baghdad by cruise missiles and the F-117 Stealth fighters were not a true reflection of what was happening elsewhere. The majority of the air raids were conducted using old-fashioned iron bombs in conditions of great danger.

Some of the most treacherous missions of all were assigned to British pilots flying Royal Air Force Tornados. The British were less enthusiastic than the Americans about standoff technology. In training, the RAF had turned daring ultralow attacks, designed to slip under enemy radar cover, into something approaching a fetish. The Americans, having lost many aircraft to small-arms fire in Vietnam, preferred to attack from higher altitudes, relying on electronic spoofing and jamming to outwit enemy radar. The British Tornados were also equipped with a specialized weapon, an airfield-busting bomb called the JP-233. The combination of its low-flying techniques and its possession of this weapon made the RAF a natural choice for the job of putting Iraq's airfields out of commission.

Each Tornado can carry two JP-233s in large dispensers under its fuselage. When the dispenser is released above a runway it spews out a cloud of mines and runway penetrators. The penetrators, stabilized by small parachutes, fall with their noses downward toward the airfield. Then, at a preset altitude, a rocket fires each penetrator down through the runway's concrete into the soil below. There it explodes, heaving up huge slabs and making the surface unfit for use. While the penetrators are doing their work, the mines are scattered throughout the rubble. Some are set to fire when touched; others remain dormant for a fixed period before they come alive. All this turns the job of runway repair into a nightmare. The RAF Tornado crews visited and revisited dozens of Iraqi airfields in the first days of the war, sometimes dropping their JP-233s along the runways, sometimes using them to cut off the taxiways linking runways to the concrete shelters. But the low-flying attacks were hazardous. Proportionally, the RAF suffered heavy losses in the war.

The euphoria of the first day's air strikes did not last for long. Nearly twenty-four hours after the opening of the bombing campaign, Iraq hit back—not at the allies with aircraft but at Israel, and later at Saudi Arabia, with missiles. In the early hours of the morning of January 18, eight Scud missiles were fired at Israel. Two landed in Tel Aviv and one in Haifa. Before these attacks the impression put out by the allied air commanders was that the Scud threat had been all but eliminated in the first strikes. President Bush, anxious to avoid the political complication of Israel being dragged into the war, had insisted that the destruction of the Scud sites in western Iraq should be a priority. Now it seemed that the attacks on the Scuds had not gone quite as well as expected.

Israel was prepared for the Iraqi attack. Saddam Hussein had said for months that the Jewish state would be his first target if war broke out. Tariq Aziz had confirmed this after his meeting with James Baker in Geneva, and the Palestine Liberation Organization's Yasser Arafat had claimed that the Iraqi missiles fired at Israel would be armed with biological warheads. In the weeks leading up to the war Israel had therefore issued all its Jewish and Arab citizens (though not the Palestinian population of the occupied West Bank and Gaza) with gas masks and syringes containing nerve-gas antidotes. Anticipating a chemical attack, the civil defense authorities had told householders not to descend to underground bomb shelters but to sit out the missile attacks in prepared sealed rooms above ground. Israelis were to continue to retreat into their sealed rooms for the remainder of the war even though, as it turned out, all of the Iraqi Scuds eventually fired at the country were armed with high explosives and not with poison gas or germs.

The Israeli defense preparations were executed flawlessly. Yet the fact that Saddam Hussein had indeed dared to carry out his threats was greeted with astonishment by some members of the Israeli general staff. They had hoped that, despite the Iraqi leader's braggadocio, the specter of Israeli retaliation would stay his hand. Israel, after all, had a more powerful missile force than Iraq. Over the years it had built an arsenal of Jericho missiles with a longer range and a bigger, more accurate warhead than Iraq's Soviet-built Scuds. Israel, moreover, was an acknowledged though undeclared nuclear power. By some American reckonings it possessed at least 100 atomic warheads, plus a smaller number of even more powerful hydrogen bombs. These seemed good enough reasons to expect deterrence to work.

However, Israel's deterrent strategy contained a logical flaw. In normal peacetime circumstances Saddam Hussein would know that an attack on Israel would bring massive retaliation. But with Iraq already being pounded around the clock by the powerful allied air forces there was little, short of nuclear retaliation, Israel could add to Iraq's pain. Like many Arab leaders, Saddam Hussein often portrayed the Israelis as demonic, inhuman, capable of perpetrating any evil. His real opinion was shrewder. He calculated that not even the Israelis would go nuclear in response to an attack by Iraqi missiles armed only with conventional warheads. And, just possibly, attacking Israel would transform the war for Kuwait into a war between Arabs and Jews, thus wrecking America's partnership with its Arab allies.

This sort or reasoning had of course been taken into account by Israel. Shortly before the war its deputy chief of staff, General Ehud Barak, was taken off normal duties and instructed to draw up plans for reacting to an Iraqi attack. Earlier in his career, General Barak had planned and taken part in some of Israel's most audacious commando raids deep inside enemy territory. He was not the sort of man to advocate an unimaginative response: the indiscriminate counterfiring of Israeli missiles at Iraqi cities, for example. Instead, a successful Israeli response would have to satisfy two conditions. It would have to be spectacular, to impress on all Israel's Arab neighbors its continuing military superiority. And it would have to be effective in silencing the Scuds.

According to American officials, who leaked the information to *The New York Times* after the war, General Barak's plan was bold to the point of recklessness. The Israelis wanted to throw an air bridge over Jordan and insert a large force of paratroopers and helicopter gunships into Iraq's western desert. They would operate there for several days from makeshift landing strips, attacking the Iraqi missile sites at the H-2 and H-3 airfields and seeking out mobile Scud launchers. Jordan's King Hussein had warned Israel that he would not tolerate Israeli flights over his territory, but the Israelis were unimpressed. Israel's air-force commander had already issued a blunt warning that if Jordan tried to intervene, Israel would immediately destroy the Jordanian air force.

And yet the Israeli retaliation never came. From the moment the first Scuds hit in Tel Aviv, Israel found itself basking in the world's sympathy and besieged by pleas to show "restraint." Luckily, this first Iraqi salvo caused no fatalities, even though it demolished apartment buildings and inflicted scores of injuries. Israel's defense minister, Moshe Arens, quickly promised that Israel would fulfill its prewar promise to strike back. But the low casualty toll gave Yitzhak Shamir, the Israeli prime minister, time to weigh his options. He was more cautious than Arens.

Israel had every right to hit back, as well as a strong incentive: the need to show that no Arab country could attack Israeli cities with impunity. On the other hand, Israel had as much reason as the Americans did to make sure that the war against Iraq was not turned into an Arab-Israeli war. If Israel kept its head down long enough it would be able to watch the allies demolish the Iraqi war machine without Israel itself having to fire a shot in anger. The American Patriot missile, an anti-aircraft weapon modified to destroy missiles, had meanwhile begun to score dramatic hits on Iraqi Scuds fired at Saudi Arabia. When Bush promised to rush additional Patriot missiles to Israel, together with their American crews, Shamir's mind was made up. Unless Iraq escalated by attacking with chemical warheads, Israel would stay out of the war.

The Israeli decision was motivated by a military as well as a political calculation. In one of the few big intelligence blunders of the war, the Israelis and Americans had underestimated the Scud threat. They thought Iraq had only two ways of launching Scuds: from fixed sites and from the special mobile launchers supplied by the Soviet Union. In fact the Iraqis had been more inventive. Before the war they bought a fleet of ordinary flatbed trucks, which were then fitted with erector frameworks that could be used once as a Scud launcher. They had more launchers, and more of the missiles themselves, than anyone suspected. The maximum estimate General Schwarzkopf had before the war was forty-eight, and just before the air campaign that figure had been reduced to eighteen. By the time he had destroyed sixteen, he was, he said later, "feeling pretty good." In fact, as Schwarzkopf explained, the Iraqis had something like fifteen battalions of fifteen launchers, which multiplies to 225 Scuds. All this meant that not even General Barak's plan would necessarily have eliminated the threat. Again, it suited Israel to pretend that it had a good military answer, while leaving the battle against the Scuds to the allies.

Saddam Hussein's attempt to bring Israel into the war was a failure, which had the unintended consequence of strengthening Israel's political standing in the Western world. However, the attacks on Israel did help Iraq's war effort in a roundabout way. The campaign against the

Scuds, which President Bush described as "the darndest search-and-destroy mission in history," was a major diversion from the main business of Central Command's war. General Schwarzkopf, making light of the problem, said he would rather brave bombardment by Scuds than an electric storm in southern Georgia. In strictly military terms he was right. Except for one incident late in the war, when one missile killed twenty-eight American soldiers in a barracks in Dhahran, the Scuds claimed few victims. But the political need to keep Israel out of the fighting meant that a high proportion of missions planned for targets in Kuwait and southern Iraq had to be canceled in favor of attacks against Scuds. The search for the launchers was never a complete success. Iraq continued to fire Scuds at Saudi Arabia and Israel until the last days of the war.

I f the Scud attacks were an unpleasant surprise, the performance of the Iraqi air force delighted the allies. During the first week, the Americans fired some 240 cruise missiles, about a quarter of their entire stock, at targets inside Iraq. Stealth fighters paid nightly visits to Baghdad, suffering no losses. (Though antiaircraft fire shot down four RAF Tornados, and forced the British to suspend low-level attacks for a while.) Yet, despite all these allied moves, the Iraqis failed to produce an effective counterpunch. At first Iraqi pilots tried quite often to get their aircraft airborne. The first week's uneven result—nineteen Iraqi aircraft shot down in air-to-air combat for no allied losses—soon persuaded them to stay on the ground. The tally of allied aircraft shot down by ground-based missiles and artillery in the first week was a fraction of what had been expected. The nearest the Iraqi air force came to taking an initiative was on January 25, when two Iraqi Mirages tried to launch an attack on allied ships in the Gulf. Both were shot down, by a single Saudi F-15 fighter.

It was soon apparent to Lieutenant General Charles Horner, the American general in charge of the allied air campaign, that Saddam Hussein's air force was going to sit out this phase of the war on the ground. This enabled him to scale back his "offensive counter-air" attacks on Iraq's airfields and to unleash more missions against the Iraqi army, its command posts and supply lines. He could not, though, ignore the latent menace the Iraqi air force still represented. In the first week only a score of its airplanes

had been destroyed on the ground. The Iraqis' best machines were stored inside concrete shelters, and many others were concealed under bridges or in residential areas well away from their bases. A few had fled to airfields in northern Iraq, out of range of many allied aircraft. The danger of these Iraqi aircraft breaking out to attack allied ships or ground forces later in the war had to be guarded against. The Israelis, in particular, feared that Iraq might use its low-flying SU-24, a modern bomber equivalent to the Tornado, to attack Tel Aviv with chemical bombs. A few of these, penetrating Israeli defenses, would be able to wreak more havoc than a flock of Scuds.

As a result, General Horner ordered a methodical attack on the Iraqi shelters. These were strong structures, but could be busted open by direct hits with 2,000-pound bombs. Iraq's far-northern air bases were to provide no sanctuary either, once American F-111 aircraft began to operate out of Turkey's NATO airbase at Incirlik. Gradually, as General Horner's confidence grew, allied tanker fleets shifted their refueling efforts further north, enabling the fighters to extend their combat air patrols over the whole country.

Unable to survive either in the air or on the ground, many Iraqi pilots made a startling decision. From the second week of the war onward, small groups of Iraqi aircraft began to dash eastward for the Iranian border. Some crash-landed and at least three were shot down by allied aircraft. Eventually, however, more than 130 Iraqi airplanes, ranging from transports to MiG-29 fighters, had found refuge with their former enemies. Iraq's motive was a puzzle; and a worry for General Horner. One theory when the escape flights started was that the air force had tried to launch a coup against Saddam Hussein, and that the conspirators had fled to Iran when the coup failed. But as growing numbers of planes made their escape, it became clear that this was an organized effort. Iran had declared its neutrality, but was no friend of the Americans. Had Saddam Hussein made a secret agreement under which his air force could swarm out of Iranian bases and attack the allied fleet in the Gulf? Or was he merely trying to save his air power from certain destruction, so that he could get it back after the war?

In the event, no attack was launched from Iran, and the Iranians did not return the aircraft to Saddam Hussein even after the cease-fire. The dash to Iran may simply have been the only thing Iraqi air commanders could think of doing when they realized the extent of their inferiority in the air. The problem was not only that they were hopelessly outnumbered; they were outclassed technologically as well. Saddam Hussein had boasted that his pilots had been trained to perform their missions even if their radio communications were jammed. However, waging a modern war in the air depends on being able to absorb and analyze vast amounts of information and then distribute orders instantaneously to individual pilots.

General Horner could coordinate his campaign with the help of ten AWACS radar aircraft—five American and five Saudi. Each was capable of detecting any aerial activity in a radius of up to 300 miles. The AWACS, however, is much more than a flying radar. It carries a team of air controllers who can monitor the positions of hundreds of enemy aircraft and orchestrate the movements of allies. The British, French, Italian, and Canadian flyers working with the Americans had practiced alongside AWACS in NATO exercises; many of their planes were fitted with data links that could receive orders in midmission to switch targets or respond to new threats. The Arab air forces had to take orders by voice over radio, but nonetheless worked well in coordination with AWACS. All this added up to what military men call a "force-multiplier": a way to make the overall power of the allied air campaign much greater than the sum of its parts.

The Iraqis, by comparison, were flying blind. They started the war with plenty of ground-based radars and data links, but these were among the first targets to be hit. Indeed, one of the opening moves of the air war was carried out not by the American air force but by its army, which used eight Apache helicopters to destroy a pair of vital early-warning stations in western Iraq with Hellfire missiles. Other radar stations were attacked by Wild Weasels, or located by RC-135 electronic-warfare aircraft and attacked by teams of special forces flown to their targets by helicopters with silenced rotors. After six days of fighting, General Colin Powell was able to show reporters a graph depicting a 96 percent decline in Iraqi radar emissions. Some radar stations survived, but their Iraqi crews decided to stay alive by keeping their equipment turned off.

General Horner had always been confident that he would rout the Iraqi air force. Having done so, the big question in Central Command's mind was how much damage allied air power could inflict on the Iraqi army. The air war settled into a routine that was to continue for five weeks. In a typical twenty-four-hour period the total number of sorties (completed missions by one aircraft) would run to as many as 3,000, or about 120 every hour. More than half were flights by tanker and reconnaissance aircraft, or by fighters providing air protection. But a typical daily workload would include around 900 bombing missions, carried out not only by the all-weather aircraft

that had launched the first attacks but also by bombers that could only fly by day, such as America's A-10 Warthog tank-busters and the French and British Jaguars. American B-52s, with bomb loads of thirty tons an aircraft, joined the attack, flying from bases in Diego Garcia and from Britain.

The effort, measured in sorties flown and bombs dropped, was enormous. But history is littered with great preparatory bombardments that failed. In 1916, at the battle of the Somme, the British artillery drenched nineteen square miles of the German front with 21,000 tons of high explosive before mounting its infantry attack. When at last the infantry went in, the German defenders were still alive. They inflicted 60,000 casualties on British troops in the first day of the battle. In the Second World War, air-force commanders made extravagant claims about the ability of air power to defeat armies in the field, but their hopes were almost always confounded. In that war, however, only about 3 percent of the bombs dropped from the air hit their targets. Unofficial estimates (though this is fiercely argued) indicate that some 20–25 percent of conventional bombs dropped in Kuwait and Iraq during Desert Storm hit their targets, and that more than 80 percent of the precision weapons did.

The allied air forces had three main types of precision weapons at their disposal. One was the Paveway laser-guided bomb, actually a set of fittings which is clamped on to an ordinary bomb so it can waggle steering fins and guide its fall toward a target illuminated by a laser beam. To hit the target the pilot must hurl his bomb into an imaginary "basket," an area within which the bomb can respond to the laser spot. As it has no propulsion of its own, Paveway's range depends on the altitude at which it is launched, but it is of the order of fifteen miles. The job of pointing the laser beam can be done by the aircraft dropping the bomb, by a companion aircraft, or even by an infantryman with a laser-designator on the ground. A second precision weapon, the GBU-15, is also an attachment to an ordinary bomb. Like Paveway it has no propulsion of its own. In its nose it carries a television camera that transmits its signal to a display in the pilot's cockpit. The pilot designates the exact point he wants the bomb to hit and then launches the bomb. Without further instructions from the pilot, the bomb steers its fall toward the designated spot (although the pilot can correct its flight if it starts to stray).

The third main weapon, the Maverick missile, has a huge warhead capable of destroying tanks and hardened bunkers. As it has its own propulsion, it can be launched from low altitudes. The missile has an infrared sensor and can see warm objects, such as tanks or trucks, which are hotter than the surrounding desert even when their engines are off. When Mavericks were attached to America's swarms of A-10 Warthog tank-busting aircraft, which have no radar, they gave this daytime bomber a way to operate at night. The pilots could use the infrared head of their missiles to locate targets that they could not see visually because of haze, bad weather, or darkness.

From the very beginning of the air campaign these and other kinds of precision weapons, together with a vaster tonnage of "dumb" bombs, rained upon Iraqi targets night and day. Towards the end of the second week, the terrible truth was beginning to dawn on Saddam Hussein. While his army, airfields, cities, and power stations were taking a beating, allied losses of pilots and aircraft had been insignificant. Except for firing his Scuds ineffectually at Israel and Saudi Arabia, he had not yet found a way to hit back. That would not matter if the allies were showing signs of launching their land forces at Iraq's formidable defenses. But General Schwarzkopf seemed in no hurry to start the "mother of all battles." His divisions were being held well back in the Saudi desert, conducting maneuvers and providing photo opportunities for an army of disgruntled reporters. Before the war, commentators

had talked about a week or ten days of "softening up" from the air before the ground war started. What, though, if the bombing continued for weeks on end? Somehow, Iraq needed a way to gain the initiative.

On Tuesday, January 29, President Bush went to Capitol Hill to deliver his annual State of the Union message to Congress. He received a rapturous welcome, and was interrupted by applause many times during his speech. The war, he told the assembled congressmen, was "on course." Iraq's ability to sustain the fighting was being systematically destroyed. Half a world away, on the Kuwaiti-Saudi border, the Iraqi army was intent on proving him wrong. That night—to universal astonishment—its tanks and troop carriers poured across the border and occupied the coastal town of Khafji, about six miles inside Saudi Arabia.

Khafji was the biggest town in the border area. But it had been abandoned by its residents, and, in accordance with General Schwarzkopf's philosophy of keeping his men out of artillery range, it was lightly defended. Although the Iraqi attacking force was small—it had fewer than 100 armored vehicles and about 2,000 men—it quickly overran the town and took up defensive positions among the deserted buildings. Eleven American marines were killed (by "friendly fire") in an engagement further west. Reading the battle from his war room in Riyadh, General Schwarzkopf evidently concluded that this was not a serious attempt to punch through the allied lines. For political reasons, the job of recapturing the town was given to untested Saudi and Qatari soldiers, helped by some American marines and missile-firing attack helicopters. After two days of heavy fighting, Khafji was back in Saudi hands. The allies took more than 500 prisoners and

destroyed scores of Iraqi tanks and troop carriers.

General Schwarzkopf, inimitably, called the attack on Khafji "about as significant as a mosquito on an elephant." That understated its impact on Iraqi morale. The battle was trumpeted in Baghdad as a famous victory and set off wild rejoicing among Saddam Hussein's admirers in Jordan and the Arab countries of North Africa. It showed that Iraqi soldiers still had some fire, if not a lot of food, in their bellies. In strategic terms, however, General Schwarzkopf was right. The point of the attack, if it was not simply a publicity stunt, was presumably to carry the war to the allied ground forces and inflict heavy losses. But the raiding force was far too small to present a real threat to the allied deployment and so lure General Schwarzkopf into starting his land campaign prematurely. There is some evidence that the Iraqis intended to reinforce their initial success with extra tank forces. The reinforcements were destroyed by allied aircraft before getting as far as the border.

The recapture of Khafji came sixteen days into the air war. By then General Horner's planes had flown 35,000 sorties and achieved many of the allies' strategic aims. Iraq's nuclear-research facilities and chemicals-weapons factories had been destroyed. The supply routes between Iraq and its garrison in Kuwait had come under repeated attack. These raids, and the destruction of scores of bridges, cut to a trickle the prewar flood of trucks and tankers down the highways from Baghdad. Virtually all of Iraq's oil-refining capacity had been knocked out, as had dozens of power plants. Most Iraqi city dwellers were having to make do without telephones, electricity, or running water. In the northern Gulf more than forty Iraqi warships or patrol boats had been sunk or damaged. Millions of leaflets had been showered over Iraqi positions in Kuwait, promising humane treatment to surrendering soldiers. The world's newspapers, inevitably, were awash with speculation about the timing of "G-Day," the moment when the war would shift to the ground. Surely it could not be much longer now?

It could. Ultimately the air campaign was to last for five weeks—longer than even its planners anticipated—before the land battle began. One cause of delay was unseasonably bad weather over both Kuwait and Iraq. Another was the unexpected difficulty of tracking down the Scuds. But the main reason was the Americans' determination to wait until they were sure that the Iraqi army was close to collapse before running the risk of engaging it on the ground.

In previous desert wars it had been easy enough for superior air forces to find and destroy tanks moving in columns through the sand. B-52s could cut great pathways of destruction through the desert, killing exposed soldiers and shaking the morale of those who survived. Finding individual tanks, spread out and buried in sand revetments with their engines turned off, was a different matter. This required identifying individual targets, learning how to distinguish between real tanks and dummies, and attacking with an appropriate weapon. At first, the allied pilots made slow progress, but gradually new tactics were evolved. A squadron of F-16 pilots dubbed the "Killer Scouts" was given the full-time job of circling over the battlefield for hours at a time to search out hidden tanks and call in strikes by other squadrons. Toward the end of the war, attacks like these were reportedly knocking out some 200 tanks a night.

In truth, however, allied intelligence was having enormous difficulty measuring the effectiveness of the air campaign. One reason is that on the most basic question—the size of the Iraqi army inside the Kuwait Theatre of Operations—there were important differences of opinion within the intelligence community.

During the autumn, following the consolidation by Iraqi troops of their conquest of Kuwait and the beginnings of their building of the fortified line in the south, allied intelligence agencies were giving journalists "deep background" briefings indicating that up to 400,000 Iraqi troops were deployed. In early 1991 this figure was increased to some 540,000. Later, General Schwarzkopf began to equivocate. Although he still maintained that the enemy had started with an army "over 500,000 strong," his story started to crumble under the hammering of simple questioning and simple arithmetic.

If, as was claimed, there had been 200,000 soldiers in the front lines and some 50,000 prisoners were taken, where were the other 250,000 or so men? Answer: a very large number of dead and a huge number of desertions. But, a few days into the land war, it became obvious that there was nothing like the number of dead in the trenches that would have been necessary to balance the books, and that the number of Republican Guards trapped in the north was nothing like 250,000. In short, the army that the allies were to attack the last week in February was substantially smaller than 540,000. By mid-March, American intelligence officials were downgrading their estimates to around 300,000, and some officials speculated privately that the number was closer to 200,000. With all their modern reconnaissance and intelligence-gathering equipment, how could the bean counters have got it this wrong?

Nobody knows for certain. Part of the answer undoubtedly lies in the propensity of all military men to overestimate enemy strength. But another part of the answer may lie in the legacy of the Vietnam war and the method used to build up a picture of the enemy force, known as the order of battle (OOB). Because it is difficult to count individual men, the standard method of accounting is by units. Once a particular enemy formation is identified (by prisoner interrogations, communications intercepts, captured documents or whatever), and its general location established, the unit is entered into the official enemy OOB; its strength is then taken as being the standard strength of that unit for that army, unless there is positive evidence to the contrary. For example, if a given brigade is known to have only two battalions, only two battalions' worth of men are counted. However, there is no easy way of cutting the manpower estimate to compensate for the effect of desertions and casualties.

During and after the Vietnam war an acrimonious debate among American intelligence officials was prompted by some officers who applied these kinds of corrections to try to obtain a better picture of the enemy. There had long been a dispute between the military intelligence men in Vietnam and the Central Intelligence Agency about how many enemy troops were in South Vietnam, the CIA maintaining a substantially higher estimate. Following the Tet offensive in early 1968, in which a huge number of enemy soldiers and guerrillas were killed, the dispute erupted spectacularly. The problem was that the military officers had downgraded the "book value" of many North Vietnamese units as well as their estimate of guerrilla forces as a result of these huge casualties.

This convinced the CIA that there was a military conspiracy to falsify the accounts for political reasons. The argument broke out into the open years later in the libel case between CBS television and General William Westmoreland, a trial that left many intelligence officers with the impression that tinkering with enemy strength figures can cause trouble. This may well have been one of the lessons of the Vietnam war that was taken too much to heart. In the Gulf the estimates of troop strength were apparently based solely on the notional strengths of known units, with no serious effort made to apply commonsense corrections. Journalists who asked at the daily briefings in Riyadh how many Iraqis had been killed were told dismissively that the army was not getting into the "body count" game. As a result, the strength of the Iraqi army in the Kuwait theater was almost certainly overestimated, which may also mean that the air war went on a little longer than necessary.

It was not the only intelligence failure. On February 12, the American air force made one of its most visible mistakes of the war. A bunker in Baghdad, which allied intelligence had identified as a military control center, was hit with lethal accuracy by two laser-guided bombs. The people inside, however, were civilians, not soldiers. Several hundred were killed by the blast and subsequent fire. Western television crews, rushed to the scene by their Iraqi government minders, broadcast grisly pictures of the carnage around the world. The Americans stood obstinately by their claim that the bunker had indeed been used for military purposes. They blamed the Iraqis for having put innocent civilians in harm's way. Whatever the truth of the matter, the tragedy renewed calls for an early end to the war. The bunker was hit while an important Soviet visitor, Yevgeny Primakov, was visiting Baghdad. By this time, too, Saddam Hussein recognized that he was losing the war. If he was looking for a diplomatic way out, this was an opportunity.

Three days later he tried to seize it. On February 15, Iraq produced a peace offer: the first in which it appeared to accept the need to withdraw from Kuwait in compliance with Resolution 660. But the rambling statement, broadcast in the name of the Revolutionary Command Council, came with a tangle of strings attached. One string was the old idea of "linkage" with Palestine. Another was that if Iraq accepted Resolution 660 the other eleven resolutions passed by the Security Council would be abolished. The statement demanded the cancelation of Iraq's debt and the withdrawal of all the troops and equipment brought into the Gulf by the Americans and other countries "taking part in the aggression." President Bush's rejection of these conditions was prompt. It was, he said, a "cruel hoax." Until Iraq agreed to all the demands set out by the United Nations, and started a massive and visible withdrawal, the war would continue without a pause.

The diplomatic door, once it had been pried open, was difficult to slam shut. In Moscow, President Gorbachev was coming under mounting criticism from Soviet army hardliners appalled at the free hand he had given America and its allies in a war 250 miles from the Soviet border. When Tariq Aziz, the Iraqi foreign minister, visited the Soviet capital on Monday, February 18, he found Gorbachev eager for an opportunity to act the mediator. Within hours, Soviet diplomats came up with a peace plan of their own. Aziz was dispatched home to Baghdad to try it out on his boss, while details were transmitted secretly to the United States. Under this plan Iraq would leave Kuwait unconditionally, with no more nonsense about "linkage." But the timing of the Iraqi army's withdrawal was not specified, and when two thirds of its troops were out, all Security Council measures against Iraq, including sanctions, would be withdrawn.

On Tuesday, while Tariq Aziz was on his way home (overland, for fear of air attack), Bush said tersely that the Soviet plan fell well short of what was required. It was an understatement. In fact the Americans were livid, fearful that Soviet mediation would give the Iraqi dictator a face-saving exit from Kuwait before the ground forces could administer the *coup de grace*. Once again, though, it looked as though Washington would be let off the hook by Saddam Hussein himself. Hussein had not yet said that he would accept the Soviet proposal. On Wednesday, with Aziz in Baghdad, clashes along the front line in Kuwait intensified. By Thursday, Aziz was expected back in Moscow with Saddam Hussein's answer. The world held its breath. Everyone now knew that if the plan were rejected by Iraq the ground war would surely begin. Finally, at midday Washington time, the answer came, or appeared to come. It took the form of an uncompromising speech on Baghdad radio by Saddam Hussein himself.

The speech, which lasted thirty-five minutes, seemed designed to prepare Iraqis for the coming battle. The Iraqi president told his people that by spurning his peace offer of the previous week the Americans had made Iraqis "more patient and steadfast," and surer of winning. There was, he said, "no other course except the course we have chosen, except the course of humiliation and darkness." When the translation reached the White House it was greeted with relief. Once again the Iraqi leader was squandering a chance to earn a reprieve, just as he had in the Baker-Aziz showdown in Geneva a month earlier. Marlin Fitzwater, a White House spokesman, feigning regret, told reporters that the speech left "little room for optimism." Then, less than nine hours later, came stunning news from Moscow. Vitaly Ignatenko, Gorbachev's spokesman, strode jubilantly into the briefing room of the Novosti press center and announced that after two hours of talks Tariq Aziz had agreed to accept an eight-point peace plan.

This caused ill-disguised irritation in Washington. The new plan was an improvement on its predecessor, but it would give the Iraqis three full weeks to withdraw their forces. Nor would Iraqi troops have to start their pull-out until a formal cease-fire had been declared. And the plan still said that by leaving Kuwait, Iraq would free itself from all of the other demands of the Security Council, including the demand that it should pay reparations for the damage it had caused. Accepting the plan would have meant letting Saddam Hussein wriggle out of Kuwait with much of his army still intact and having to face no additional punishment for his invasion. The question in Washington was not whether the Soviet proposal should be accepted, but how to turn it down without causing a head-on clash with Gorbachev.

This time, Bush's advisers decided to grab back the initiative. Instead of waiting for yet another round of bargaining between the Soviets and the Iraqis, the U.S. would set out its own terms for avoiding a land war, and couple it with an ultimatum. On Friday the 22nd, after a night of feverish telephone calls to other members of the alliance, Bush accordingly announced that Saddam Hussein would have until noon (Eastern Standard Time) on Saturday to begin his withdrawal. Kuwait City would have to be evacuated within forty-eight hours, the rest of Kuwait within a week. Although the allies would exercise "restraint" by not attacking retreating forces, there was to be no formal cease-fire while the Iraqi army withdrew.

Not even Saddam Hussein would be able to present this as anything other than a surrender, and nobody in Washington, or in General Schwarzkopf's war room in Riyadh, expected him to try. Inside Kuwait, the Iraqis were already setting fire to scores of oil wells, as Hussein had threatened they would. American aircraft were concentrating more strikes on Iraqi front-line positions, using napalm and monstrous "fuel-air explosives" (clouds of explosive gas spread over the battlefield and then detonated) to burn up fuel trenches and flatten mine fields. In many places, special forces and marines were already across the border, rounding up prisoners and marking paths through mines. The final act in the liberation of Kuwait was about to begin.

The 100 Hours

Schwarzkopf's "Hail Mary" offensive play sets up the Iraqis for the kill

The Iraqi soldier is a prodigious digger. The fortifications which sprouted along the Saudi border soon after the invasion of Kuwait were gradually deepened and improved until they became a truly formidable military obstacle. By mid-January a fortified line coiled virtually continuously from Kuwait City south along the Gulf coastline to Saudi Arabia, and thence westward along the border some seventy-five miles beyond the western tip of Kuwait. The line consisted of deep antitank ditches and a series of "berms," massive sand walls reaching up to forty feet high in some places. To these obstacles were added dense barbed-wire entanglements and extensive mine fields. In some sectors military engineers also laid out pipelines to flood some of the ditches with gasoline or diesel oil. The idea was to turn the antitank ditches into a wall of flames when allied forces started to breach them.

Behind this chain of obstacles the Iraqis had deployed scores of thousands of troops, perhaps as many as twenty divisions. These were not Iraq's best soldiers. Many were new conscripts with little training, or older men who had fought against Iran and had been recalled. But they dug themselves into deep bunkers and foxholes and possessed large numbers of tanks and artillery pieces. Their instructions were to bring allied forces struggling through the defensive barrier under withering direct fire, delaying the advance and inflicting as many casualties as possible. Further back, in northwest Kuwait, was a second line of defense consisting of several armored divisions. The mission of these divisions was to move quickly to seal any breach in the fortified line, or cut off any allied force that might try to outflank the western end of the line. Again, these forces were not Iraq's best, but in the right conditions they could be doughty fighters. One such unit had launched the attack on Khafji.

Iraq's final line of defense, stationed well back in southern Iraq, consisted of five divisions of the Republican Guard. This was the Iraqi army's strategic reserve, the sharp sword that would swing into action against any major force that succeeded in penetrating the defensive shield. For five weeks this force had been attacked relentlessly by allied bombers, but the allied commanders were not certain how much the sword had been blunted. Central Command, drawing on pilots' reports as well as satellite photography, thought that some of the divisions had lost as much as a quarter or even half of their strength. The CIA was less optimistic.

Central Command drew up several plans for the recovery of Kuwait. One, the simplest, would have entailed a massive thrust directly north into the heart of the Iraqi defenses around Kuwait City. This was rejected by the joint chiefs. The plan they eventually approved was a more subtle flanking attack, designed to exploit the allies' superior mobility and the difficulties Iraqi armored formations would encounter if they were forced to move in the open under attack from the air. According to this plan two Saudi-led formations and a corps of two American marine divisions would indeed attack north directly into Kuwait. But this would be a feint. The main striking force would execute a grand sweeping maneuver well to the west of Kuwait and through Iraq itself. Then it would turn right to trap and attack the Republican Guard divisions in their bases near Basra. At the hinge of this gigantic pincer there would be another strike force—Britain's 1st Armored Division (including the "Desert Rats" of the 7th Armored Brigade)—whose job would be to break through near the western end of the barrier and destroy Iraq's second-echelon armored divisions inside Kuwait.

To divert attention from the main thrust in the west, Central Command concocted an elaborate deception plan. Its aim was to persuade the Iraqis that the American marines intended to make a vast amphibious landing on the Kuwaiti coastline near Kuwait City. Fear of this landing, it was hoped, would become a magnet drawing the attention of the Iraqi army away from the real threat shaping up nearly 200 miles away inland in the desert. As part of the deception, two marine brigades, with nearly 20,000 men, were embarked in ships well before G-Day (the start of the ground war) and brought far up into the northern Gulf. To give the impression that a landing was imminent, allied minesweepers stepped up their activities. Two American battleships, the *Missouri* and the *Wisconsin*, pounded the shore with their sixteen-inch guns. Long before the ground war started, news reporters and television teams had been invited to watch the marines rehearsing seaborne landings. General Schwarzkopf was gratified to see newspaper commentaries everywhere discussing the importance of the allies' ability to land marine forces near Kuwait City.

The deception was continued inland. Britain's 1st Armored Division, with 250 Challenger tanks, extra artillery, and special expertise in breaching fortifications, had spent most of its first months in the desert attached to the American marines. Those marines who were not embarked on ships were being kept well east, near the coastline. To strengthen the impression that the main threat to the Iraqis in Kuwait would come from the south and east, not the west, allied commanders misinformed the press that British tanks were still operating alongside the American marines. In fact the 1st Armored Division had been moved westward as an independent force, to form the hinge between the allies' two main thrusts. Tape recordings of a British live-firing exercise were broadcast from a position some fifty miles to the east of the British assembly points, in the hope of outfoxing Iraqi radio monitors. In the last few days before the opening of the ground attack, several front-line units sent their artillery regiments to fire off much-televised cross-border barrages miles away from the real positions of their parent divisions.

If this did not confuse the Iraqis, nothing would. Yet the boldest part of the deception plan—which General Schwarzkopf later called his "Hail Mary play"—was yet to come. For months before the war, the main allied armored divisions were aligned immediately south of the Kuwaiti border, helping to nurture the impression that the offensive would come straight up into Kuwait from the south. "Every morning when I would get out of bed," General Schwarzkopf said later, "the first thing I would do is go look at the map to see where his forces were and whether or not he was in fact extending his forces further out on the right flank. And I'll tell you, the day we executed the air campaign, I said 'We gotcha' because by then it was impossible for them to reinforce that flank...

I knew then I could move the forces without him being able to see them." In the days before the ground campaign began, the divisions that had been concentrated in the east were sent racing westward into the desert, well beyond the fortified line the Iraqis had painstakingly built around Kuwait. The rapid movement of tens of thousands of fighting vehicles and supply trucks required an enormous logistical effort. Only one good road, the Saudi Tapline route parallel to the Iraqi border, was available. Adding to the logistical nightmare was General Schwarzkopf's insistence that a full sixty-days' worth of food, water, and ammunition should also be moved west. If the left hook through Iraq ran into strong resistance, he did not want his armored divisions running short of the supplies they would need to sustain a prolonged battle.

In any previous war, a deception strategy of this kind would have stood little chance of succeeding. The huge armored columns moving west through the desert and kicking up vast clouds of dust would have been instantly spotted from the air, prompting the defenders to reposition their own forces to meet the attack. Five weeks into the air war, however, the Iraqis had stopped trying to fly reconnaissance over the border, and even their ground patrols had given up attempts to find out what was happening inside Saudi Arabia. The handful of Iraqis who did manage to cross the border seemed more intent on surrender than intelligence-gathering. By the allied launch time, 4 A.M. in the morning of February 24, the Iraqis were still braced for a ground attack straight into Kuwait from the south, combined with a marine landing on the coast. In fact the bulk of the allied army, some ten divisions, had just gone inland and was no longer facing Kuwait at all. It was preparing to drive deep into the lightly defended desert of Iraq itself.

The forces with the task of delivering the left hook were divided into two groups: the American VII Corps, under the command of Lieutenant General Fred Franks, and the American XVIII Corps under Lieutenant General Gary Luck. VII Corps was the armor-intensive heavy hitter, with the job of finding and destroying the Iraqi Republican Guard divisions, the backbone of Saddam Hussein's war machine. Under its command were three American armored divisions (the 1st Cavalry, 1st Armored and 3rd Armored) and the 1st Infantry, a mechanized division which is known throughout the American army as The Big Red One after its red insignia. Britain's armored division, which the Iraqis thought was still operating alongside the marines near the coast, was also attached. This gave General Franks a grand total of about 1,500 tanks, most of them the powerful M1A1 Abrams, with a

120mm gun and an astonishing cross-country speed of nearly forty-five miles an hour. To scout ahead and protect his flanks he had the 2nd Armored Cavalry Regiment and the 11th Aviation, a helicopter brigade.

If VII Corps was the heavy hitter, General Luck's XVIII Corps, further west, was the long-distance runner. Its mission was to perform a massive loop north through the desert and east into the Euphrates valley. There its job would be to cut the road links between Basra and Baghdad. That would both prevent any Iraqi reinforcements moving south from the center of the country and cut off any Iraqi units trying to escape toward Baghdad from the VII Corps' armored fist. General Luck's men would have to move with lightning speed, and the composition of his helicopter-rich force was configured accordingly. It included the 82nd and 101st Airborne divisions and a mechanized division, the 24th Infantry. Two helicopter brigades (12 Aviation and 18 Aviation) were also attached, as was France's 6th Light Armored Division. For reconnaissance, General Luck had the 3rd Armored Cavalry Regiment. A division of Saudi and Pakistani troops was strung out westward of his positions along the Saudi-Iraqi border to guard against any intrusion by fleeing Iraqi troops.

To the east of these two American corps was an Arab force (Joint Forces Command North) with two armored divisions and one mechanized division, plus several independent armored and commando brigades. These units included Egyptians, Saudis, Syrians, Pakistanis, and some reconstituted elements of the Kuwaiti army. Another Arab force (Joint Forces Command East) was stationed on the coast immediately south of Kuwait, with about five brigades of troops from Saudi Arabia, Oman, Kuwait, and the United Arab Emirates. Sandwiched between the two Arab forces, under the command of Lieutenant General Walter Boomer, were the American marines' 1st and 2nd Divisions, reinforced by the "Tiger Brigade" of the army's 2nd Armored Division. The 4th and 5th Marine Expeditionary Brigades were embarked on their amphibious ships in the Gulf.

G-Day was set for February 24, a Sunday. By the previous day all five commands—the two left-hook forces facing the Iraqi border and the three commands lined up south of Kuwait—had moved silently into position, ready to launch the attack. For the Iraqis, the first sign that something was about to happen was a change of emphasis in the allies' air campaign. For weeks beforehand, the Iraqi army inside Kuwait had been pummeled around the clock from the air. Sometimes these raids were so heavy that allied soldiers ranged along the Kuwaiti border could

hear the roar of falling bombs and feel the ground shake. On Saturday, however, the air attacks that had been directed at roads, bridges, and the positions of the Republican Guard inside Iraq virtually ceased, and some 80 percent of allied air sorties were concentrated in a thunderous aerial blitzkrieg over the Iraqi front-line positions inside Kuwait. At 4 A.M. on Sunday morning, the blow fell.

The French were the first big force to move. The light tanks of General Michel Roquejeoffre's French division ploughed across the Iraqi border at the far left of the allied deployment and charged north. The French objective was a desolate place called As Salman, about ninety-five miles inside Iraq, where there was an airfield and a crossroads. By taking As Salman, the French would be securing the left flank for an advance toward the Euphrates valley by the tanks and heli-borne troops of General Luck's XVIII Corps. Patrols had reported that As Salman was protected by about 10,000 soldiers of the Iraqi 45th Division, but the defenders were taken by surprise and resistance was light. The French troops, helped by a brigade of American paratroopers from the 82nd Airborne, made rapid progress, encircling As Salman by nightfall. It fell after a brief battle in which the French used missile-firing Gazelle helicopters to destroy a number of Iraqi tanks. The outcome was one-sided. General Roquejeoffre lost only two dead and twenty-five wounded while capturing some 2,500 Iraqis and bringing As Salman under allied control.

At first light on Sunday, soon after the French had crossed the border, more than a hundred troop-lifting helicopters from the American 101st Airborne Division, the "Screaming Eagles," started lifting off from positions slightly to the east. Within a matter of hours, 2,000 assault troops had been ferried at high speed over more than fifty miles of Iraqi desert to a scrap of emptiness that was soon to be known throughout XVIII Corps as Cobra base. The surrounding desert had been searched and strafed in advance by Cobra and Apache helicopter gunships, to make sure that the handful of Iraqi defenders in the area would not put up a fight. They didn't. As soon as the airborne troops landed they dug themselves into foxholes and set up a defensive perimeter with TOW antitank missiles. Low-flying Chinook transport helicopters hauled in howitzers and tens of thousands of gallons of aviation fuel. But there was no Iraqi counterattack. A few bewildered Iraqi infantrymen emerged from bunkers to give themselves up. By evening a convoy of several thousand troops from the rest of the division linked up with the advance party at Cobra base after driving overland through the desert.

Cobra was only the first of several refueling bases that the 101st Airborne plonked down by air deep in the Iraqi rear. "This is air assault history in the making," one of the Screaming Eagles' brigade commanders had told reporters before the attack began. Certainly, nothing in the Iran-Iraq war had prepared the Iraqi army for the abrupt arrival of powerful enemy airborne forces hundreds of miles behind their front line. On Monday evening, before the Iraqis could respond, the Screaming Eagles used their helicopters to leapfrog forward over the desert for a second time. More than 60 Blackhawk helicopters, loaded with about 1,000 troops, flew just above the desert floor deep into the Euphrates valley. This time the division set up a firebase, Objective Gold, close to Highway Eight, the main road linking Baghdad and Basra, and along which the Iraqis would have to retreat if they wanted to escape. The Iraqi army was being cut off and prepared for the kill, just as General Colin Powell had said it would be at a Pentagon briefing a month earlier.

By comparison with what was to come, the movements of the French and the Screaming Eagles were light jabs. But their rapid success and the feebleness of the opposition persuaded General Luck that it was safe to unleash the heavier forces belonging to XVIII Corps earlier than

planned. On Sunday afternoon, therefore, the 3rd Armored Cavalry Regiment and the 24th Infantry Division rumbled across the Iraqi border, churning up vast clouds of sand. The 24th's commander, Major General Barry McCaffrey, had been told to drive as fast as possible across open country toward the Iraqi town of An Nasi-riyah, which straddles Highway Eight on the Euphrates. Once it mounted the highway, the division would turn east and head toward Basra from the direction of Baghdad—the last direction, it was hoped, from which the Iraqi Republican Guard was expecting to be attacked. General McCaffrey had nearly 300 Abrams tanks under his command, as well as a powerful force of artillery and his own detachment of Apache helicopters. After two days of hard driving and fighting across the desert, the division's tanks had reached the Euphrates, overruning the Talil and Jalibah airfields and shooting up more than a dozen MiGs stranded on the runways.

In most wars, the original plan seldom survives contact with the enemy. Yet General Luck's long-distance run around the far west of Kuwait had not only gone to plan, it had gone much faster than planned. Central Command decided to bring the whole timetable forward. The VII Corps under General Franks started its war a little later, at 6 P.M. on Sunday. With the left flank secured by General Luck's corps, three of General Franks' armored divisions—the 1st Armored followed by the 3rd and the 1st Cavalry, plus the 2nd Armored Cavalry Regiment—poured into Iraq from a position several miles to the west of the end of the Iraqi fortified line and motored north at high speed. The mission of XVIII Corps had been to reach the Euphrates and prevent the Republican Guard divisions from escaping. General Franks' principal job was to perform a shallower left hook around Kuwait and destroy them. The Guard divisions were not VII Corps' only worry, however. General Luck also had to take account of the possibility of the Iraqi second-echelon armored divisions inside Kuwait stabbing due west and cutting through the vast logistic trains that were beginning to straggle out in the desert behind the advancing American tanks.

To stop any such counterattack, General Franks was counting on the British. Major General Rupert Smith's 1st Armored Division with its hundreds of Challenger tanks had been detached from the American marines and was now deployed close to the junction between the Iraqi, Kuwaiti, and Saudi borders. The British division's orders were to attack north and then turn sharply east and destroy the Iraqi armored reserve inside Kuwait. Unlike the divisions that had crossed the border further west,

GROUND CAMPAIGN:
THE FIRST 48 HOURS

Saddam Hussein wanted his "mother of all battles" to be as bloody as possible. He expected the allies to try to breach the fortifications his army had thrown around southern Kuwait. But the allied air offensive had rendered him blind to a vast westward movement of U.S., British, and French forces, who plunged deep into the lightly defended Iraqi desert. Airborne troops swooped into the Euphrates valley, seizing control of the main highway. The Iraqi army sat uselessly in its bunkers while the trap closed.

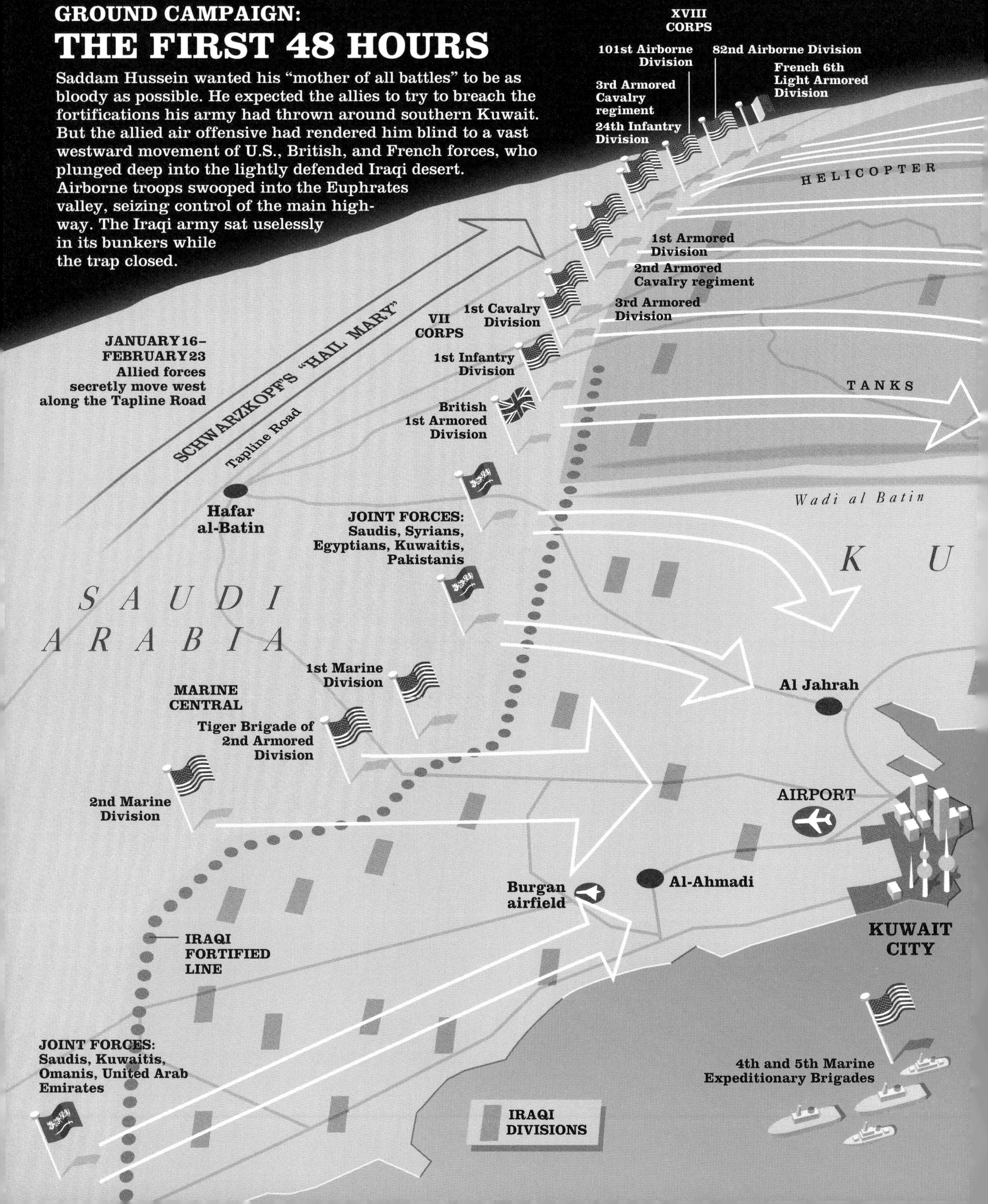

XVIII CORPS

101st Airborne Division

82nd Airborne Division

3rd Armored Cavalry regiment

French 6th Light Armored Division

24th Infantry Division

HELICOPTER

SCHWARZKOPF'S "HAIL MARY"

JANUARY 16– FEBRUARY 23 Allied forces secretly move west along the Tapline Road

Tapline Road

1st Armored Division

2nd Armored Cavalry regiment

3rd Armored Division

VII CORPS

1st Cavalry Division

1st Infantry Division

TANKS

British 1st Armored Division

Hafar al-Batin

JOINT FORCES: Saudis, Syrians, Egyptians, Kuwaitis, Pakistanis

Wadi al Batin

K U

S A U D I A R A B I A

Al Jahrah

1st Marine Division

MARINE CENTRAL

Tiger Brigade of 2nd Armored Division

AIRPORT

2nd Marine Division

Al-Ahmadi

Burgan airfield

KUWAIT CITY

IRAQI FORTIFIED LINE

JOINT FORCES: Saudis, Kuwaitis, Omanis, United Arab Emirates

4th and 5th Marine Expeditionary Brigades

IRAQI DIVISIONS

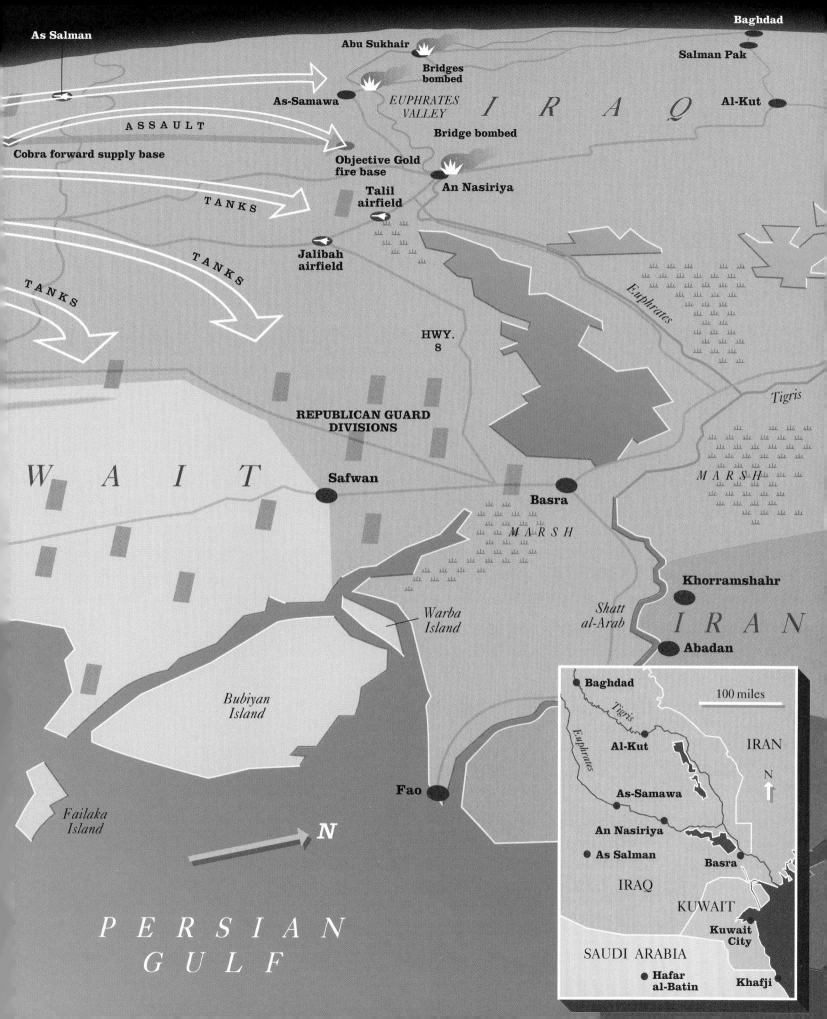

As Salman

Abu Sukhair

Bridges
bombed

As-Samawa   EUPHRATES   I R A Q   Baghdad
                    VALLEY   Salman Pak

ASSAULT   Al-Kut

Cobra forward supply base   Bridge bombed

                    Objective Gold
                    fire base   An Nasiriya

TANKS   Talil
               airfield

TANKS

Jalibah airfield

TANKS

TANKS   Euphrates

                    HWY.
                    8   Tigris

          REPUBLICAN GUARD
          DIVISIONS   M A R S H

W A I T

          Safwan   Basra

                              M A R S H

                                                            Khorramshahr

                                          Warba   Shatt   I R A N
                                          Island   al-Arab

                                                            Abadan

                    Bubiyan
                    Island

          Failaka
          Island   N

                    Fao

P E R S I A N

G U L F

Baghdad   100 miles

          Tigris   IRAN

          Al-Kut   N

Euphrates

          As-Samawa

An Nasiriya

As Salman   Basra

          IRAQ

                    KUWAIT

SAUDI ARABIA   Kuwait
                      City

          Hafar
          al-Batin   Khafji

GROUND CAMPAIGN:
THE FINAL PHASE

When the final hammer blow fell, many Iraqi soldiers were still expecting the main attack to come from the south, and from U.S. marines at sea. Instead, an entire corps of American tanks billowed out of the desert behind the Republican Guard, forcing them into battle in the desolate sands west of Basra. Iraqi forces retreating toward Baghdad drove smack into an American mechanized division and were shot to pieces, while marines and allied forces rolled over the Iraqi defenses south of Kuwait City.

Tapline Road

Hafar al-Batin

Wadi al Batin

K U

S A U D I
A R A B I A

JOINT FORCES:
Saudis, Syrians,
Egyptians, Kuwaitis,
Pakistanis

2nd Marine Division

Al Jahrah

MARINE CENTRAL

Task Force "Ripper"
pushes through airport
to Kuwait City

AIRPORT

MARINE CENTRAL

Burgan airfield **Al-Ahmadi**

KUWAIT CITY

IRAQI FORTIFIED LINE

JOINT FORCES:
Saudis, Kuwaitis,
Omanis, United Arab
Emirates

4th and 5th Marine
Expeditionary Brigades

IRAQI DIVISIONS

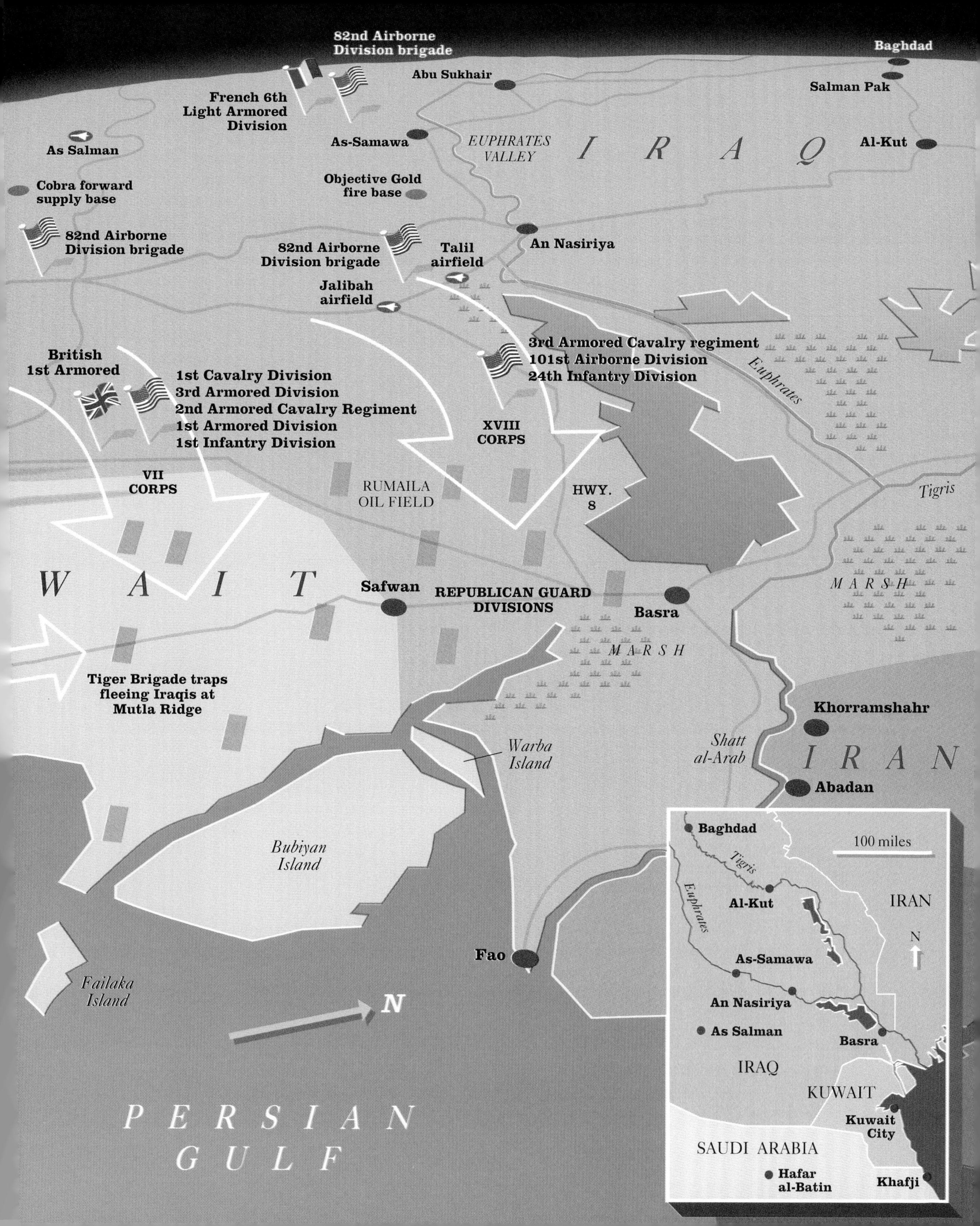

82nd Airborne
Division brigade

Baghdad

French 6th
Light Armored
Division

Abu Sukhair

Salman Pak

As Salman

As-Samawa

*EUPHRATES
VALLEY*

I R A Q

Al-Kut

Cobra forward
supply base

Objective Gold
fire base

82nd Airborne
Division brigade

82nd Airborne
Division brigade

Talil
airfield

An Nasiriya

Euphrates

Jalibah
airfield

3rd Armored Cavalry regiment
101st Airborne Division
24th Infantry Division

British
1st Armored

1st Cavalry Division
3rd Armored Division
2nd Armored Cavalry Regiment
1st Armored Division
1st Infantry Division

XVIII
CORPS

VII
CORPS

RUMAILA
OIL FIELD

HWY.
8

Tigris

W A I T

Safwan

REPUBLICAN GUARD
DIVISIONS

Basra

M A R S H

Khorramshahr

M A R S H

*Shatt
al-Arab*

I R A N

Tiger Brigade traps
fleeing Iraqis at
Mutla Ridge

*Warba
Island*

Abadan

*Bubiyan
Island*

Fao

*Failaka
Island*

N

P E R S I A N

G U L F

Baghdad

100 miles

Tigris

Al-Kut

IRAN

Euphrates

As-Samawa

N

An Nasiriya

As Salman

Basra

IRAQ

KUWAIT

Kuwait
City

SAUDI ARABIA

Hafar
al-Batin

Khafji

however, the British division would have to negotiate the dense fortified line that the Iraqis had looped around Kuwait and extended a short way along the Iraqi-Saudi border. To speed the British on their way, therefore, General Schwarzkopf had decided that the breach in this line would be opened not by the British but by The Big Red One, the American 1st Infantry Division. Once the American division had opened a gap in the line it would be expected to hold a perimeter on the north side so that the British tanks could dash through unmolested.

The complex breaching operation went as smoothly as an exercise. Artillery hammered the Iraqi positions behind the line. Helicopters lifted squads of reconnaissance troops over the top of the sand walls to block counterattacks. Bulldozers broke gaps in the outer berms and tanks moved through them, taking up firing positions. Combat-engineering tractors fired 200-yard-long "snakes" of high-explosive charges across the mine fields, then blew them up to clear away mines and barbed wire. After each firing the tractors followed the scorch marks left by the snakes and fired again, repeating the procedure until they had crossed the mine fields. Behind them came engineers on foot, marking safe tracks for the armor to follow. Bundles of pipes were dumped into the antitank ditches to enable armor to cross. For the wheeled vehicles that came later, the engineers bulldozed sand on top of the pipes to form a flattish roadway. In all, The Big Red One cut sixteen lanes through the barriers and mine fields over a front of about two miles. Its own armored and artillery units fanned out north of the barrier. They met only slight resistance, taking about 1,700 mostly willing prisoners within the first few hours.

By Monday afternoon the bridgehead was secure, and

the British tanks rolled through on schedule. At 11 P.M. they made contact with the enemy, overrunning a battalion headquarters and capturing its commander. During the night the British force sliced through Iraq's 12th Armored Division and completed the turn toward the east. Now it was advancing into Kuwait itself on a front about thirty miles wide, looking for the Iraqi 6th Division. But the British tankers, like so many allied units in this war, soon found themselves underemployed. The worst casualties inflicted on them were the result of a "friendly fire" accident. An American A-10 Warthog attacked two British Warrior fighting vehicles, killing nine men. As for the Iraqis, the possibility of using their armored reserve to strike west at the ever-lengthening supply tails of VII and XVIII Corps never seemed to occur to them. Just possibly, the Iraqi high command's eyes were still fixed where General Schwarzkopf's deception plan had drawn them: on the threat from the south.

General Boomer, the senior marine commander, may not have been happy about his amphibious forces being used for a feint, deprived of the chance to make an opposed landing, as they had trained to, in the area of Kuwait City. But the substantial marine force deployed on land between the two Arab commands south of Kuwait was determined to grab a slice of the action. Even before the official start of the land offensive, its two divisions had been nibbling at the front line, slipping combat patrols across the berms to attack isolated Iraqi positions. Here and there the patrols met fierce resistance, but they also discovered that allied air raids had already knocked big gaps in the Iraqi defenses. Overnight on February 22–23, two days before G-Day, several hundred men from the 1st Marine Division reportedly moved into Kuwait under cover of a drenching rainstorm. They penetrated undetected for twelve miles, then dug themselves into foxholes on the edge of the Iraqi sand berm.

On the morning of G-Day, both marine divisions launched themselves across the border in two northward thrusts toward the international airport south of Kuwait City. The Iraqi units nearest the border surrendered immediately. "Their morale is about boot-top level," said one marine officer. But by the time the American columns of tanks, personnel-carriers, and infantry reached the second Iraqi berm, the Iraqis were firing back. Several American tanks were knocked out crossing the berm, but Apache and Cobra gunships and marine jump jets pounced on the defenders and the advance continued. That night Iraqi mechanized forces launched a counterattack from the Burgan airfield. In this battle, the marines claim to have destroyed four Iraqi T-62s and taken 3,000 prisoners. Three of their own M60 tanks were damaged. The marines' most violent battle did not come until Wednesday, when the tank forces reached the airport. It fell only after a fierce battle.

The marines' advance was supported on each flank by friendly Arab forces. On the left flank Egypt's 3rd Mechanized Division punched a multilane breach through the Iraqi fortifications. On the coast, the Arab forces under Joint Forces Command East advanced in a long column across shallow dunes toward Kuwait City. This column included Kuwaiti troops, crossing back into their country for the first time since August. They stopped briefly at the border to pose for photographs and fire off a few celebratory rounds.

The sheer weight of the opening allied attacks on Sunday took the Iraqis by surprise. In Washington, Cheney had called for a news blackout while the ground fighting continued. But at 4 P.M. on Sunday an ebullient General Schwarzkopf emerged from his war room in Riyadh to give a brief progress report to journalists. After ten hours of battle, he said, allied forces had taken more than 5,000 prisoners and suffered remarkably light casualties. All the objectives set for the first day had already been achieved and the attack was progressing "with dramatic success." The Iraqis' main response was verbal. From Baghdad, Saddam Hussein hit back with what one British newspaper called "the mother of broadcasts," calling on his beleaguered soldiers to show the enemy no mercy. "Fight them with your faith in God," he declaimed, "fight them in defense of every free and honorable woman and every innocent child, and in defense of the values of manhood and the military honor... Fight them because with their defeat you will be at the last entrance of the conquest of all conquests. The war will end with... dignity, glory, and triumph for your people, army, and nation."

Unsurprisingly, this appeal made no visible impression on the fighting. In the final days before the start of the land war, the average Iraqi soldier in Kuwait must already have had a dismal view of the outcome of any battle. Nine days before G-Day, the Iraqi leadership had publicly accepted the need to withdraw from Kuwait. Three days before G-Day Saddam Hussein had broadcast a warlike speech on Baghdad Radio. Yet several hours after that speech Tariq Aziz had accepted the Soviet peace plan. This bewildering sequence of developments can have left the Iraqi soldiers with little incentive to fight and die for a nineteenth province which their leadership had already offered to give up. All along the front demoralized and often hungry infantry units were surrendering after the first few shots of battle. One group of barefoot Iraqis

marched disconsolately across the Saudi border holding wooden poles to which they had tied white undershirts. They told their Egyptian captors that they had not eaten for two days. Their own officers had told them surrender was their only chance of staying alive.

On Monday, therefore, some twenty-four hours after his "fight them" speech, Saddam Hussein zig-zagged again. Sunday's appeal to his soldiers to fight for dignity, glory, and triumph was abruptly superseded. Now, inexplicably, Baghdad Radio announced that the Iraqi armed forces had been ordered to withdraw "in an organized manner" to the positions they held on August 1, the day before invading Kuwait. "This is regarded," the broadcast said, "as practical compliance with Resolution 660." For months before the land war started, a unilateral Iraqi withdrawal that gave Saddam Hussein a chance to quit Kuwait and save his army had been regarded by some officials in Washington as a "nightmare scenario." But the idea that the Iraqi army could make an organized withdrawal under fire on that Monday night was nonsense. By then General Luck already had forces astride Highway Eight, and the armored divisions commanded by himself and General Franks were closing the trap on the Republican Guard. Inside Kuwait itself the Iraqi army was in full flight, or surrendering in thousands. By telling his soldiers to leave their prepared defensive positions and withdraw as if no war was happening Saddam Hussein was as good as ordering his own army's destruction. Why?

By Monday, presumably, the Iraqi dictator had abandoned all hope of winning the military contest for Kuwait. His paramount interest was in finding a way to arrange his own political survival after the war was over. He had refused to withdraw unconditionally before fighting the "mother of all battles" because the humiliation at home might have been too great. Pulling out after only one day of battle, on the other hand, was a tempting compromise. His retreating soldiers might well be massacred, but Bush would come under renewed Soviet pressure to bring the war to an end. At home, meanwhile, Hussein would be able to tell his people that Iraq had been stabbed in the back by superior forces while complying with the Security Council's main demand.

Baghdad Radio's Monday broadcast did indeed cause

consternation in the White House. But after six months of preparation, President Bush was not going to let a brilliant victory slip between his fingers. On the battlefield, everything was going much faster than planned, and with hardly any casualties. At the U.N., pressure for a cease-fire was muted. Although the Soviets had expressed "regret" at the outbreak of the land war, they were not thumping the table and demanding that it stop. In these circumstances there was little reason to halt the campaign in its tracks. On Tuesday morning, therefore, Bush stepped onto the White House lawn and called Baghdad's broadcast of the night before an "outrage." The Iraqi army, he said, was not withdrawing, it was in the middle of a rout. Nor was Hussein giving up Kuwait voluntarily. "He is trying to save the remnants of power and control in the Middle East by every means possible." At General Schwarzkopf's headquarters in Riyadh, the signal was received loud and clear: the war would go on.

Like many of Bush's wartime decisions, this one took courage. Although the war was going well, the Republican Guard divisions had not yet been engaged. Many of their tanks had been destroyed by bombing, but the remainder might still be able to kill a lot of Americans in the forthcoming armor-to-armor battles. Some Iraqi soldiers in the north were indeed fighting well. Iraqi special forces near Talil airfield in the Euphrates valley had resisted for several hours. Bush knew that stopping the war on Tuesday would probably mean that Kuwait would end up liberated at a negligible cost in allied lives. Fear of casualties was dominating Washington's thinking about the war. But stopping prematurely would also mean a job half done. The bulk of the Iraqi army would then survive to pose a continuing threat in the future. Bush decided to risk the casualties and press on for a conclusive victory.

As Wednesday dawned in the Middle East, the allied military position could hardly have been more favorable. The French division and the 82nd Airborne Division were in blocking positions slightly south and west of As Samawa, on Highway Eight about halfway between Baghdad and Basra. To their east the next stretch of the highway, from As Samawa to An Nasiriyah, was controlled by the 101st Airborne Division. Further east still, the highway was controlled by General McCaffrey's 24th Infantry along with the 3rd Armored Cavalry. These forces made up a solid anvil, blocking the Iraqi army's escape routes. In the desert fastnesses south of Highway Eight, General Franks' armored divisions were moving into position for the massive hammer blow intended to destroy what remained of the Republican Guard.

The battle was easier than anyone had expected, not least because even on Wednesday the Iraqis appeared to have little idea about the allied movements in their rear. When the tanks of General McCaffrey's 24th Division started clattering along Highway Eight their commanders soon met columns of retreating Iraqi tanks. The Iraqi commanders, however, had no idea that their highway to safety was now under the control of the American army. Instead of moving in fighting order on their tracks, the T-72 tanks had been loaded on flatbed transporters and were being hauled in single file up the highway. They were blown apart by the 24th Division, and the Iraqi crews fled into the surrounding marshland. About twenty miles west of Basra, the Hammurabi Division tried to deploy for a set-piece battle but was broken up by a combination of long-range artillery fire and air attacks before its tanks could get within range of the Americans.

VII Corps had meanwhile finished its march north. Now, parallel to the Rumaila oil field, General Franks swung his divisions east. Rick Atkinson, a journalist with *The Washington Post*, described the armored formations sweeping toward the Republican Guard as "a steel wedge sixty miles wide and one hundred twenty miles long." Cavalry scouts in helicopters flew a dozen miles ahead of the column, while hundreds of supply trucks spread out in the desert behind it. Heavy rains and thousands of tracked vehicles had churned the desert into a soup, but the Abrams tanks and Bradley fighting vehicles moved swiftly forward.

The Iraqis' most feared weapon was their artillery. Yet the Iraqi gunners achieved virtually nothing in the face of this attack. One reason was simply the speed of the American advance. Time and again Iraqi shells hit positions which American armor had left ten minutes earlier. But the main reason was the effectiveness of the Americans' counter-battery fire. Moving forward with the American armored divisions were units equipped with the latest artillery-locating radar. These machines enabled their operators to measure the trajectory of incoming shells within seconds and plot their point of origin. The relevant coordinates were then flashed immediately to the allied artillery units, who opened up with counter-battery fire, or to helicopter gunships and fixed-wing bombers which pounced on the Iraqi batteries from the air. Many Iraqi artillerymen reached the conclusion that their safest course was not to open fire at all. At no point, moreover, did the Iraqis fire chemical weapons.

General Franks' first victim in this high-speed onslaught was the Republican Guard's Tawakalna Division. The Medina Division tried to withdraw, but its escape routes were cut off. In most encounters between

Abrams tanks and the Republican Guard T-72s, the Abrams came out on top. In some cases Iraqi tanks scored hits on the American machines but the shells failed to penetrate their armor. Major General Ronald Griffith, the commander of the American 1st Armored Division, claimed that his attack destroyed more than 600 Republican Guard tanks for only four of his own. But most of the destruction seems to have been wrought by artillery and air power before tank combat was joined. Despite thick dust and black smoke, scores of Apache helicopters swooped on the Iraqi armor, or popped up from behind sand dunes to fire their laser-guided Hellfire antitank missiles with amazing accuracy. One Apache pilot said he had destroyed seven Iraqi tanks with seven Hellfire missiles in a single sortie. By Wednesday evening, in the words of one participant, "there was no one left to fight."

By comparison, the liberation of Kuwait City was almost an anticlimax. From day one of the land campaign, Kuwaiti government sources had been reporting the capture of the city in a vast parachute drop. The truth was more prosaic. Small groups of American and British special forces infiltrated the city well before G-Day, but most of its Iraqi defenders decided to flee before any substantial enemy forces showed up. It was, for thousands of them, a fatal mistake. An undisciplined column of retreating Iraqis, some twenty-five miles long, soon clogged the road to Basra. It was stopped by the American Tiger Brigade and attacked immediately from the air with cluster bombs, missiles, and cannon fire. Inside Kuwait City itself, in a testament to the success of the deception strategy, allied troops later found a schoolroom that the Iraqis had turned into a command center. It contained a carefully crafted sand model, twenty-six feet by forty feet, on which Iraqi officers had marked the positions of their own forces and the expected direction of the allied attack. All the red arrows showed allied soldiers invading from the sea; all the model tanks and guns representing the Iraqi defenders were pointing that way. None was turned inland in the direction from which the city was eventually taken.

On Wednesday afternoon, General Schwarzkopf strode out of his war room to give journalists his second progress report in three days on the land fighting. It quickly became obvious that the briefing was, in effect, a victory announcement. For the first time, the general gave a detailed explanation of the deception plan. He described the great left hook Generals Luck and Franks had delivered around the west of Kuwait. Then he announced the results. Some twenty-nine Iraqi divisions had been rendered "completely ineffective." More than 3,000 of the 4,000 tanks Saddam Hussein had in the Kuwaiti theater

had been destroyed or captured. And, because the escape routes north had been cut, "you can add 700 to that as a result of the battle that's going on right now with the Republican Guard." One journalist, who thought of asking the general his opinion of Saddam Hussein as a military strategist, got this now-famous reply: "He is neither a strategist nor is he schooled in the operational art, nor is he a tactician, nor is he a general, nor is he a soldier. Other than that he's a great military man, I want you to know that."

Officially, the war was still going on while the general was speaking. But reports on the fighting had been relayed to the White House continuously during the day, and a decision in principle to cease fire had already been taken. Bush and his inner circle watched General Schwarzkopf's Riyadh briefing on television. A few hours later, at 9 P.M. New York time, George Bush went to the Oval Office to address the nation. "Kuwait is liberated," he said. "Iraq's army is defeated. Our military objectives are met. Kuwait is once more in the hands of Kuwaitis, in control of their own destiny." Seven months had passed since Saddam Hussein's army had thundered across the border and overrun Kuwait. The land battle to win it back had lasted one hundred dazzling hours.

There was a dizzying velocity to television's pictures of the war. The humdrum image of the daily briefing would suddenly explode into the celestial glow of a Patriot missile seeking to fore-

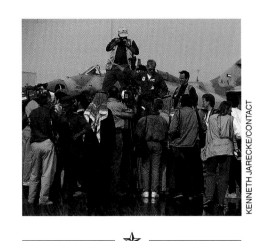

Images of

stall death. Hour after hour it was Saddam Hussein and his nodding apparatchiks, Bush and his presidential seal, the cockpit of an F-15 delivering a smart bomb, the pundits, the tank crews, the flaming oil wells, the drowned birds. Today's spectators became tomorrow's victims: The Tel Aviv families who watched Baghdad burn were themselves, within hours, in the same eye of the world as they struggled to put on their gas masks. Recollection of all this is inevitably a blur. The moving picture is less easily

War

recalled than the still photograph that isolates a moment of time. The following pages are a collection of moments that will never elude memory. They are more lastingly powerful than the strobe show of the first true television war.

Iraqi TV Taped Broadcast

———— ★ ————

Action!

It was about oil. It was about money. It was about pride. It was about arrogance. But it finally manifested itself, as wars do, with a single order, in a single act. At 2 A.M., August 2, 1990, Saddam Hussein did exactly what he had assured his Arab brothers and the world he would not: He sent the T-72 tanks of his feared Republican Guard rumbling into Kuwait. By sunset, the second-richest per-capita country in the world was his. Kuwait, he said, would become a "graveyard" if anyone attempted to redress his piracy.

How could it have happened? It happened, as wars do, because of an opportunity glimpsed, warnings unheard, duplicity unrecognized, an unfounded conviction that the political risk was worth the power to be gained.

The Iraqi invaders met no resistance. Within hours the Republican Guard began to pillage and loot Kuwait. Within days everything from tons of gold in bank vaults to living room sofas was being trucked to Baghdad as the spoils of war. Thousands of Kuwaitis were to be kidnapped, raped, tortured and murdered. The bloodshed and destruction were mindless. Among things the Iraqi soldiers wantonly destroyed—one of the oldest known copies of the Koran.

----------- ✫ -----------

Declared Saddam: Kuwait no longer exists. That nation is now the 19th province of Iraq.

PETER KURZ/GAMMA LIAISON

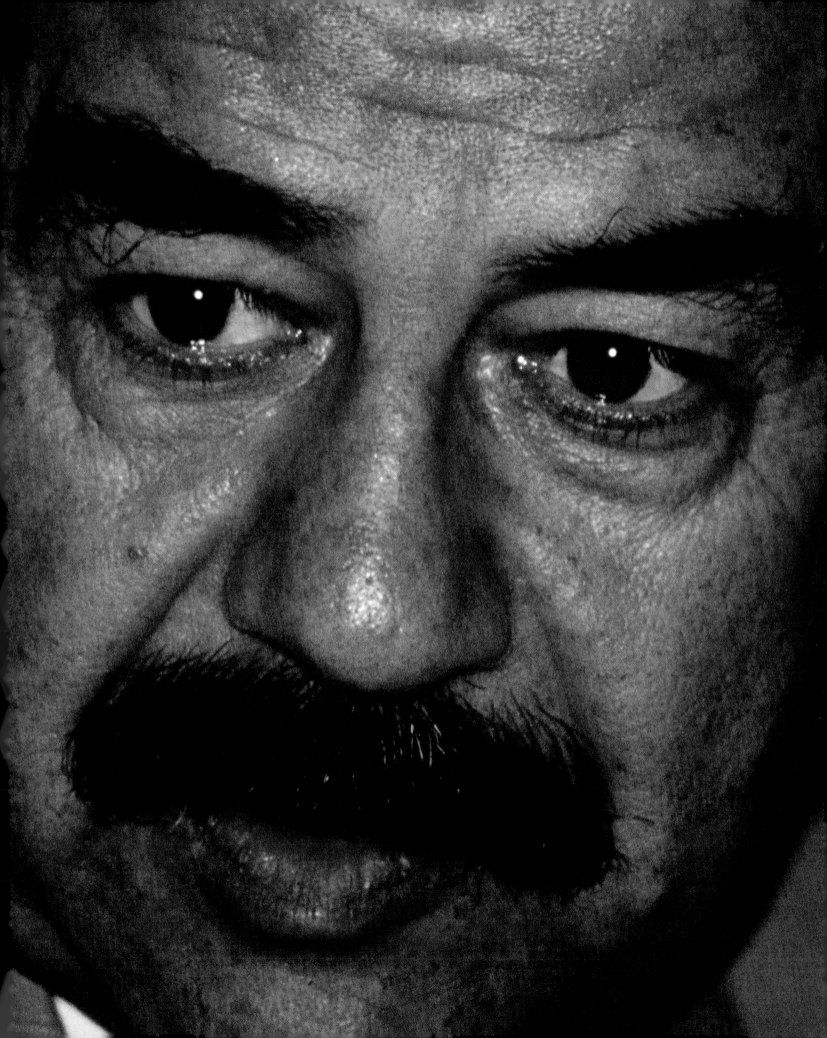

Reaction!

George Bush's answer to Iraq's "naked aggression" was a remarkable political and moral performance. Saddam Hussein had misread his foe. No wimp now, if ever, Bush chose toughness. He quickly won the support of his military and his cabinet. He then took to his telephone to rally hesitant Arab leaders. He called upon the world's democracies, and was assured of help.

Buoyed by the President, the U.N. Security Council demanded immediate, unconditional Iraqi withdrawal from Kuwait. With Saudi Arabia's nervous agreement, Bush sent 200,000 troops to defend that country's borders. In November he shocked his country—and others—by doubling that troop commitment. On January 12 Bush wrote Saddam: "Should war come, it will be a far greater tragedy for you and your country."

When Saddam failed to begin a pullout of his forces, the greatest air war in history was launched. Five weeks later the ground attacks began. In one hundred hours the war was over. The military execution had been brilliant. The political execution had been brilliant too.

Declared Bush: The acquisition of territory by force is unacceptable.... No one should underestimate our determination to confront aggression.

Saddling Up for Saudi

In the hasty, chaotic first weeks of the August deployment, marines at March Air Force Base in California board a Gulf-bound 747. Commanders knew the initial troops sent were more a token of U.S. resolve than a real threat to Saddam. For the first month of Desert Shield, one aide said, "Schwarzkopf was terrified about our vulnerability."

The Long Good-bye

Farewells to soldiers setting off for war: tableaux of love, fear, and determination as timeless as human conflict. On air bases in California, in Florida boot camps and the naval yards of Virginia, families and sweethearts kissed and wept as the troops left home. In each parting was sadness as well as a small, but defining sort of courage— the choice to face death and the unknown solely in the service of one's country.

The Mighty Military Buildup

By mid-January, the U.S. was leading a twenty-eight-nation force that numbered nearly a million. The American naval armada included two battleships, six aircraft carrier battle groups, and six nuclear submarines. Marines hit the deck of the carrier Independence *for push-ups during a break in F/A-18C Hornet flight operations.*

The Army's 1st Cavalry Division created a tent city.

The GI ration: eight bottles of water daily.

Tanks arrive in Saudi Arabia, creating a rush-hour jam.

Cluster bombs are stockpiled.

The USS Kennedy *bristles with F-14 Tomcats.*

By late August, U.S. troops drill in Dhahran.

On the Firing Line

Amassing 168 tanks and 43,000 men—including these from the 1st Staffordshire Regiment—the British would be a formidable force in the ground war.

Troops from Many Lands

Among the more than two dozen countries that sent fighting men to the Gulf was France with a force of 18,000. The aircraft carrier Le Clemenceau *arrived with forty Gazelle choppers, missiles, infantrymen, and antiaircraft artillery. At right, from the top: The 500 Islamic soldiers from Niger guarded the holy shrines of Mecca and Medina. Syria supplied 17,000 troops and 300 Soviet-built T-62 tanks. The Saudis' all-volunteer force included men from Bahrain, Oman, Qatar, and the United Arab Emirates. Eleven thousand Kuwaitis who escaped the Iraqi invasion represented their homeland. Egyptians numbered 40,000.*

JOHN GIORDANO/SABA

DIETHER ENDLICHER/WIDE WORLD

BARRY IVERSON/WOODFIN CAMP

JOHN GIORDANO/SABA

YVES DEBAY/FOTO CONSORTIUM

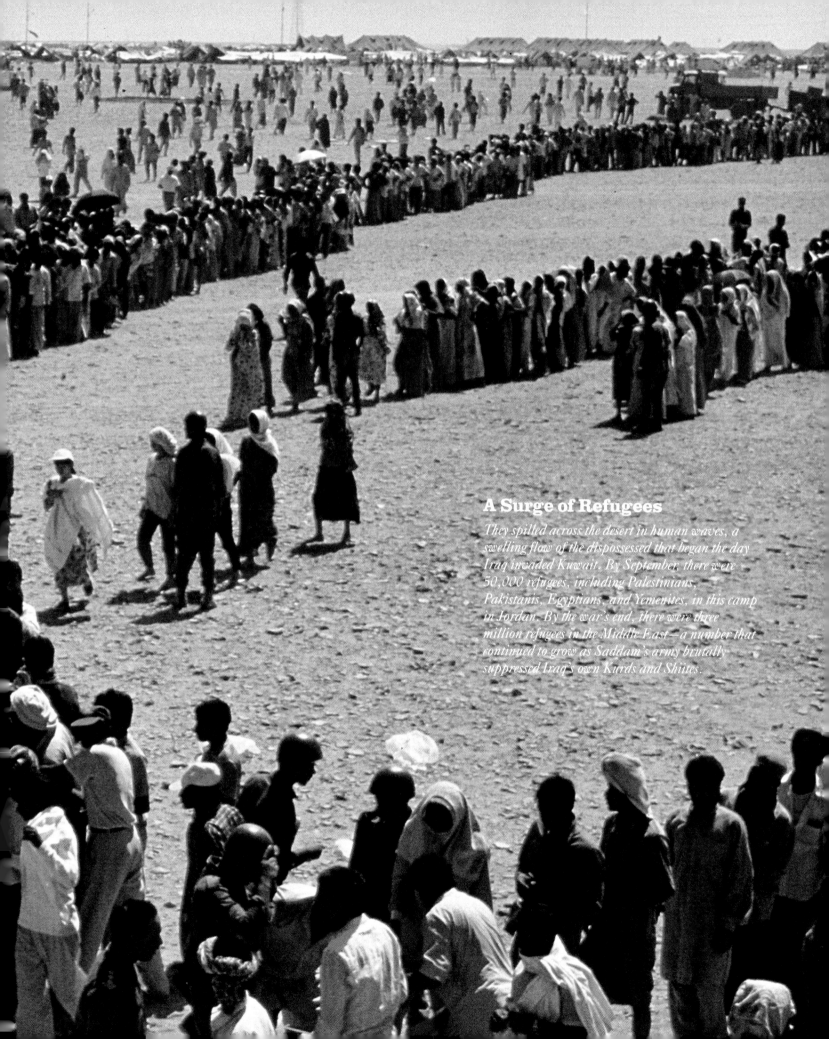

A Surge of Refugees

They spilled across the desert in human waves, a swelling flow of the dispossessed that began the day Iraq invaded Kuwait. By September, there were 50,000 refugees, including Palestinians, Pakistanis, Egyptians, and Yemenites, in this camp in Jordan. By the war's end, there were three million refugees in the Middle East—a number that continued to grow as Saddam's army brutally suppressed Iraq's own Kurds and Shiites.

AHMED A./SIPA

Capital Punishment

Kuwait City witnessed the full range of war's horrors in bloodshed and barbarism. Iraqi firing squads dealt out summary retribution to soldiers accused of crimes. Kuwaitis suffered throughout the occupation. Some saw their life's work vanish when Iraqi troops destroyed the souk (left). Those who opposed Saddam's forces paid a higher price: Mutilated and killed, the corpses of many resistance fighters were left to rot in the street. When allied soldiers re-took the city, friends could finally bury the dead.

DAVID LEESON/DALLAS MORNING NEWS/JB PICTURES

Protest and Pride

The conflict kindled deep emotions in Americans. Some questioned the need for U.S. intervention, in quiet candlelit vigils or angry demonstrations like one in San Francisco (left). Others felt the war was just and paid honor to the nation and its soldiers. More than 10,000 rallied to form a human map in Florida, and yellow ribbons bloomed like flowers. But patriotic preschoolers in Netcong, New Jersey learned also of war's cost: watching the funeral of a neighbor killed in the Gulf.

Consultations on Two Continents

In early February, moving toward the start of the ground war, U.S. leaders met in Riyadh with Saudi defense minister Prince Ibn al-Aziz. At the White House, two days before the land offensive began, George Bush and Secretary of State Baker worked out a final deadline for an Iraqi withdrawal.

**America's
Fighting
Idealist**

———— ✦ ————

Norman Schwarzkopf, the first American general to become a national hero since Eisenhower and MacArthur, was early on disparaged as "a fatherly meatpacker" and a "lunch-pail lug." His appearance is as deceptive as his military tactics that caught Saddam's armies facing the wrong way. "Gotcha!" he said then. But the tough street-talker is a well-read, sensitive man. In Vietnam he brooded long and painfully about where duty stopped and morality began. He suffered deep hurt when the sacrifices of the soldiers were repudiated by a hostile public at home. He quotes Sherman that those who invite war deserve what they get; but he is never far from tears when he thinks of the dead and the maimed. The Bible by his camp bed in the desert was well thumbed, and he often quoted a prayer attributed to Saint Francis: "Dear Lord, make us instruments of your peace." The victor of the Gulf war is a fighting man because he is an idealist. He believes freedom is worth dying for.

The General

HIS WAR IN WORDS

"Any soldier worth his salt is antiwar."

"Perhaps it is immature, perhaps it is naive, but I believe in the basic goodness of man."

"A leader establishes the ethical...environment in which the entire operation is going to be accomplished."

"When you commit military forces, you ought to know what you want that force to do."

"I never underestimate the enemy...I look at his capabilities and assume he has them until we find out differently."

"Any man that doesn't cry scares me a little bit."

"If the Iraqis are dumb enough to attack, they are going to pay a terrible price for it."

"It is not a Nintendo game; it is a tough battlefield where people are risking their lives at all times."

"Any decision you have to make that involves the loss of human life is nothing you do lightly. I agonize over it."

"It doesn't take a hero to order men into battle. It takes a hero to be one of those men that goes into battle."

"I am not being micromanaged from Washington, certainly not from the White House."

"I'm apparently not famous in Baghdad."

"We just went right around the enemy and were behind him in no time at all."

"I like to think of myself as a man of conscience."

"God loves the infantryman, and that's just the kind of weather [rain, dust, black smoke] the infantryman likes to fight in."

"The President, in every case, has taken our guidance and recommendations to heart and has acted superbly."

"I've been scared in every war I've ever been in."

"When I think of the people who were five-star generals, I can't even see myself standing in their shadow."

In his final press briefing, Schwarzkopf tartly summed up the victory in a 57-minute virtuoso performance that became a hit video. He reviewed troops with Saudi Arabia's King Fahd and faced the enemy at the cease-fire talks. The highly visible "Bear" kept U.S. casualties— ninety in actual combat— lower than those from a single bad week in Vietnam.

Operation Desert Norm

★

BY C. D. B. BRYAN

Ihave read the stories about "Stormin' Norman," the terrible-tempered "bear" who is a "pussycat" to his family. I have read how this general with the 170 genius-level IQ lulled himself to sleep in his Riyadh quarters listening to Pavarotti and Willie Nelson. I have read of his fluency in French and German; his love for the ballet and opera; and his membership in the International Brotherhood of Magicians. And I am sure, as reported, he has studied T. E. Lawrence's *Seven Pillars of Wisdom*, and that he has *The Kingdom*, Robert Lacey's acclaimed history of Saudi Arabia, on his nightstand. I especially enjoyed the account of how, at his Kuwaiti hosts' insistence, Schwarzkopf several years ago donned Arab robes and later said of the experience, "It was just like the scene in *Lawrence of Arabia* when the British officer's clothes are taken away and replaced by robes, and he waltzes into the desert, intrigued by their feel and grace. I stood in front of the mirror and did the same dance. It was wonderful." When I asked him if that quote was accurate, he laughed. "No," he said, "I didn't say I did the same dance. I mean, it wasn't exactly a dance; I *will* admit I stood there and sort of twirled around and let the robes flow."

I can see him doing that. I first met H. Norman Schwarzkopf in October 1971. He was then a thirty-seven-year-old lieutenant colonel not long back from completing his second tour of duty in Vietnam. Twice wounded, he had just been released from the Walter Reed Army Medical Center and was recuperating at home in Annandale, Virginia, with his wife, Brenda, and his two-year-old daughter, Cindy. Schwarzkopf—a large man at six feet three and a half inches and, in those days, maybe 225 pounds—looked even more huge in a cast that covered him from his hips to his shoulders.

Seventeen months earlier, on May 28, 1970, Schwarzkopf had been commanding the Americal Division's 1st Battalion of the 6th Infantry Brigade in South Vietnam's Batangan Peninsula when a portion of his battalion's Bravo Company became trapped in a mine field. Bravo's company commander and a lieutenant had both been badly wounded, and a med-evac helicopter had been called for. Schwarzkopf, airborne in his Huey helicopter with Captain Bob Trabbert, his artillery liaison officer, reached the stranded unit first and turned over his Huey to get the wounded out. Schwarzkopf and Trabbert then stayed behind.

The remainder of the patrol was still frozen in the middle of the mine field. Schwarzkopf said the young soldiers were on the edge of panic. Their commanders had been evacuated; they felt leaderless, abandoned. Schwarzkopf told them calmly that they were going to be all right, to walk back out the way they had walked in: "Watch where you put your feet, keep to your old tracks, stay calm, keep your distance."

They had begun to move again when a young soldier a dozen yards from Schwarzkopf stepped on another mine. The explosion punched the kid up into the air and injured Trabbert and Schwarzkopf slightly. They felt the impact, the pain before the young soldier even hit the ground. The boy's right leg was flapping out to one side. "My leg! MY LEG!" he screamed, and Schwarzkopf sensed the men beginning to panic again. He told them to keep still, and called to Trabbert to radio the med-evac helicopter to hurry. The private who had stepped on the mine was screaming and thrashing about on the ground. The men around him were terrified that his flailing would trigger another explosion. Schwarzkopf began inching across the mine field to reach him. He still had twenty feet to go when the private started panicking again. "I'm going to die! We're all going to die!"

C. D. B. Bryan is the author of *Friendly Fire*, about the war in Vietnam.

Schwarzkopf's legs began to shake uncontrollably. His knees were suddenly so watery that he had to reach down and grip them until they stilled. Perspiration stung his eyes. The men were watching him, waiting for him to move again. To his astonishment, Schwarzkopf said, he suddenly thought of the sign on Harry Truman's White House desk: THE BUCK STOPS HERE.

The kid was whimpering, "I don't want to die! You've got to get me out of here."

"I'll get you out," Schwarzkopf said. "Just keep still. You're all right."

Five feet...three feet...Schwarzkopf gently lowered himself across the wounded boy's body to keep him still. "I don't want you to move around," Schwarzkopf told him. "We're going to have to set that leg."

Schwarzkopf needed a splint and spotted a small, waist-high tree back where he had left Trabbert and three other men. Schwarzkopf called to them to cut some splints from the tree. Trabbert pulled out his sheath knife and passed it to one of the men. The soldier took one step toward the tree and triggered another mine.

Schwarzkopf was horrified. Trabbert had taken the full force of the explosion. His left leg was blown off, an arm broken backward so that the bone of the elbow socket showed, and a great hole was gouged in his head. He would survive, but the three other men were killed instantly.

For having crossed the mine field to rescue the wounded private, Schwarzkopf was awarded his third Silver Star. He says he had no other choice. It was his responsibility. And by being there in the mine field taking care of the boy instead of with Trabbert, his life was saved. "But you live with those things," he said. "You become terribly fatalistic in combat."

I was interviewing Schwarzkopf for *Friendly Fire*, the book I was writing about an Iowa family whose twenty-five-year-old son was killed by a howitzer shell fired by his own supporting artillery in Vietnam. Michael Mullen had been a sergeant in Charlie Company, one of the infantry companies in Schwarzkopf's battalion. I had gone to see Schwarzkopf because Michael's parents were wrongly convinced he was responsible for their son's death.

Mullen's death deeply distressed Schwarzkopf—as did the death of any soldier who served under him. In fact, twenty years ago he was clearly distressed about the entire Vietnam experience. Late that first night he said to me, "I *hate* what Vietnam has done to our country! I *hate* what Vietnam has done to our Army! The government sends you off to fight its war. It's not *your* war, it's the government's war. You go off and fight not only once, but twice, OK? And suddenly, a decision is made, 'Well, look, you guys were all wrong. You're a bunch of dirty bastards! You never should have been there!' Now this is going to make me think long and hard before I go off to war again. This is me, Norm Schwarzkopf, personally....And when they get ready to send me again, I'm going to have to stop and ask myself, 'Is it worth it?' "

It was an extraordinary comment for a young West Point lieutenant colonel with three Silver Stars. Overnight he must have realized it, too. The next morning it was one of the first things he mentioned after we had again sat down. "Let me clarify that," he said. "If I decide to remain in the service and the government orders me to go, I will go. I don't see how I can refuse unless I felt so strongly about it that my only alternative was to resign from the Army." Schwarzkopf paused for a moment. "We can get into a very subtle discussion here of conscience and duty, the Nuremberg trials, the Japanese war criminals, etc. What is moral? What is immoral? Where does duty stop and morality begin? Are we now saying that the military is supposed to question the morality of our government's commitment to war? I don't know....If we allow the military to question whether or not to go, then it seems to me we also have to look at the other side of the coin: What if the government decides *not* to go? Do we allow the military the right to criticize this decision?...See, the military is required to follow the orders given it by the government. How they pursue it is another question—and here is where you get into civilian casualties, war crimes, atrocities, ovens, and all that business....If it ever came to a choice between compromising my moral principles and the performance of my duties, I know I'd go with my moral principles. At the same time, however, I would also cease being an Army officer. I would have to resign my commission. But even at that I could be accomplishing my duty as I see it."

H. Norman Schwarzkopf was born in Trenton, New Jersey, on August 22, 1934. His father, Herbert Norman Schwarzkopf, was the son of German immigrants who spoke no English in the home. Schwarzkopf

senior graduated from West Point and, at his son's birth, was head of the New Jersey State Police, overseeing the conviction and execution of Bruno Hauptman for the kidnap-murder of Charles and Anne Morrow Lindbergh's baby. He later hosted the old radio show *Gangbusters* before returning to active duty with the Army during World War II. It is hard to know how great an influence the father had on the son, but Schwarzkopf told me, "A lot of my love of country stemmed from my father. My dad was a genuine public servant who had a deep and abiding love for his country..."

In 1946, twelve-year-old H. Norman

Schwarzkopf, with a wounded paratrooper in 1965, was shattered by the response to Vietnam.

Schwarzkopf went to Iran to join his father, who was training that country's police. (In 1953 he was instrumental in the coup that overthrew Iran's Prime Minister Mossadegh and restored the Shah to his throne.) The young Schwarzkopf lived in Iran for a year, in Germany for two years, and then in Italy for a year before he was seventeen. At West Point he wrestled and played tennis and football; he conducted the chapel choir and graduated in the top ten percent of his class of 1956 both academically (43rd out of 480) and militarily (he was a captain, the highest cadet rank one could attain). Upon gradua-

tion he was commissioned a second lieutenant and entered active duty.

In 1984, when I saw H. Norman Schwarzkopf for the second time, he was a major general in command of the 24th Infantry Division (Mech) at Fort Stewart, Georgia. Commanding an American combat division is a plum assignment. Only sixteen generals get it. Speaking of the fun of being a general, he said, "Now I can fix all those things out there in my domain that I think are broken." And then he laughed and added, "At the same time, you hope your judgment is good, because there are a lot of other generals that have gone around thinking they were fixing things, and they were just breaking them like crazy!"

We were sitting in his quarters enjoying an after-dinner whiskey, and, not surprisingly, conversation had turned to the Vietnam War. His first tour in Vietnam had been as a young captain/major assigned to the South Vietnamese Airborne Battalion as a task force adviser. It was in 1965–66, the very heat of battle, and Schwarzkopf and the Vietnamese Airborne had been in the middle of it. "We fought for almost every day of every month for thirteen months," he said. Schwarzkopf was proud of his unit, and of his own service. "I really thought we had done something good, just like George Washington," he said. "I had gone and fought for Freedom."

Upon completing that tour Schwarzkopf flew out of Vietnam practically nonstop to New York. He was thirty-two years old and in uniform—"because," he said, "I was this soldier coming home from war." But there were no parades, no crowds to greet him. The terminal was empty. He grabbed his duffel bag, walked out into the early morning fog, and hopped in a helicopter to Newark. He expected the cab driver who took him from Newark to his mother's home in East Orange to see his uniform and say, "Oh! Are you just back from Vietnam?" But the driver didn't say a thing. And when Schwarzkopf said, "Sure is great to be back in the U.S. again!" the driver didn't even ask, "Where have you been?"

By 1969, when Schwarzkopf was sent to Vietnam a second time, he was married to Brenda. He served as a battalion commander with the Americal Division and returned in 1970. "And this time when I came home," he said, "not only was I not getting greeted and flowers thrown on me and loved—except for Brenda, who was happy to see me—this time, when I came back the uniform was spit upon. Television was depicting the career military officer as "a Neanderthal," he said, "who with blind, unquestioning obedience burned villages and killed babies. And what made it so difficult was the fact that *I hadn't done any of that!*

"Everyone who went to Vietnam and came home, after it was over, has had to come to his personal accommodation for that experience," Schwarzkopf said. He compared it to undergoing surgery for cancer: "When it's all over you've got the scar, number one; and number two, you're not really ever sure that you got it all out of your system. You never know when it's going to rear its ugly head again. But if you're going to live your life, you're going to have to learn to live with that. But I have to tell you, I was undergoing tremendous peaks and valleys to arrive at my own accommodation for my life. There were times when I was tempted to just bail out and go build myself a cabin in the wilderness...."

A turning point came for Schwarzkopf in the fall of 1983, when he was serving as the deputy task force commander for the American invasion of Grenada. Flying toward the island in his army helicopter, he saw a crudely lettered message painted in red on a soccer field and fully expected it to say, "Yankees Go Home." But he was surprised to see that it read "God Bless America!" And upon his return to Fort Stewart, he was moved by a small group gathered at the airfield to welcome him. The army band was there; his wife, the children, and his black Labrador "Bear"; as were his enlisted aide, some of the privates he shot skeet with, some members of his staff, and their wives and children. "Johnny was coming home from the war again and I had expected to come home just the same way I came home from war the last two times: no big deal. It was going to be routine. But the airplane landed, the band was out there, and there were big signs saying, "Welcome Home," and I walked out of the airplane and everybody started cheering and my wife and kids ran up and hugged

me, and I didn't understand what was going on! Isn't that crazy? Do you see what I'm saying? But I've got to tell you, when it finally dawned on me, it was probably one of the greatest thrills I have ever had in my entire life." That night Schwarzkopf told me that if he had returned from Grenada to an American press that had been violently anti-Grenada, an American people that were violently anti-Grenada, he didn't think he could have handled it.

"When you commit military forces," Schwarzkopf said, "you ought to know what you want that force to do. You can't kind of say, 'Go out and pacify the entire countryside.' There has got to be a more specific definition of exactly what you want that force to accomplish. In Grenada the objective was very clear....It is very important," he added, "that if we commit again to any kind of battle that we are sure we understand the ramifications of what happens if we *do* accomplish our objectives. It is conceivable that we could want to demonstrate our resolve in an area, but be unable to arrive at a set of military objectives that would satisfactorily accomplish them. And if that's the case, then you should not commit the military. There may be other ways to do it....We should not just throw them in 'to show our resolve' because it could be that we end up losing, failing in our initial objective, which was to show resolve."

Unlike in Vietnam, the military objectives in the Gulf were clearly defined. If the Iraqis did not unconditionally withdraw from Kuwait, the coalition was to eject them. "One of the reasons why we are pursuing the battle the way we are," Schwarzkopf told me a few weeks before the ground war started, "is because it's very important we understand that we don't want to win the war and lose the peace. That's why we're in this coalition. That's why the rules of engagement we have are such. That's why what we are trying to accomplish is, I would say, limited in objective rather than unlimited from the standpoint of wreaking mass destruction upon the entire nation of Iraq."

Norm Schwarzkopf had been preparing for the Operation Desert Storm command all his life. With him in Saudi Arabia was the 24th Infantry Division he formerly led. It is a mechanized division specifically designed for the sort of open terrain tank warfare it faced in the Gulf. I had asked him whether, if the war ended without his having the

opportunity to utilize his ground forces, he would be disappointed.

"Not in the least!" he said vehemently. "I don't want to kill one more American! I don't want to see one more American die—be it from an accident or from battle. There's no blood lust on the part of myself or anybody else around here. What we want to do is to accomplish the objectives of this whole thing, get it over as quickly as we can, and get back home. And I tell you, that's the attitude of everybody from the top general down to the lowest private." His response made me think of the soldiers in that previous war and how often that phrase about getting it over as quickly as possible and getting back home surfaced in their letters. There is one big difference, though. "The troops' morale over here is very, very high," Schwarzkopf told me. "They feel good about what they're doing over here."

Later, I rooted out a parcel Schwarzkopf had sent me after I saw him at Fort Stewart seven years before. Among its contents, I remembered, was a bound series of lectures on generalship given as part of an Art of War colloquium held at the U.S. Army War College at Carlisle Barracks, Pennsylvania. The collection opened with the following quote from an A. von Bogulawski:

"For what art can surpass that of the general—an art which deals not with dead matter but with living beings, who are subject to every impression of the moment, such as fear, precipitation, exhaustion—in short, to every human passion and excitement. The general not only has to reckon with unknown quantities, such as time, weather, accidents of all kinds, but he has before him one who seeks to disturb and frustrate his plans and labours in every way; and at the same time this man, upon whom all eyes are directed, feels upon his mind the weight of responsibility not only for the lives and honor of hundreds of thousands, but even for the welfare and existence of his country."

In a *Washington Post* interview from Saudi Arabia, Schwarzkopf said, "Every waking and sleeping moment, my nightmare is the fact that I will give an order that will cause countless numbers of human beings to lose their lives. I don't want my troops to die. I don't want my troops to be maimed. It's an intensely personal, emotional thing for me. Any decision you have to make that involves the loss of human life is nothing you do lightly. I agonize over it."

I believe him. □

Gas Lines Above an Ocean of Oil

A lesson in desert warfare learned from Rommel: An army lives and dies by its fuel supplies. Allied success rode on efficient logistics. Marine personnel carriers queue up for gas south of the Kuwaiti border; fuel tankers and supply trucks of the 1st Armored Division cross the Saudi desert.

The Die Is Cast

The U.N. deadline for Saddam to begin his withdrawal from Kuwait was set: noon, New York time, on January 15. The moment came and went. It was now apparent that Saddam would not budge. Thirty hours later, the allied bombardment of Iraq began.

A Tomahawk missile roars off the 50-year-old battleship Wisconsin *for a target in Iraq 600 miles away.*

Desert Storm's Thunder and Lightning

The thirty-three-day air campaign—the most intensive ever waged, and the first to win a war—comprised more than 100,000 missions, dropping ten times the explosive power of the Hiroshima blast. Early tactical strikes wiped out Iraqi radar and air bases, then U.S. commanders called in fifty mighty B-52s. After weeks of bombardment, just 20,000 Iraqi troops in the region were able to fight.

Brains with Brawn

Matching ferocious firepower with technical prowess, the allies' air weaponry ranged from the AH-64 Apache helicopter—bristling with a 30mm chain gun, laser-guided missiles, and 70mm Hydra rockets—to unarmed planes like the E-2C Hawkeye, identifying friend and foe from as far away as 300 miles.

The Arsenal

Marshaling the tools of war on land, air, and sea, the conflict justified the

Pentagon's faith in high-tech weaponry and proved the mettle of old hardware.

The radar-invisible Stealth fighter was as ominous as its name. Whether observed at takeoff or refueling, it was a true specter of the war.

Technology

SGT JEFF WRIGHT/U.S. ARMY

F/A-18 Hornet

The single-seat, carrier-based strike fighter was a workhorse in the Gulf. Equipped for night fighting, the $24-million Hornet serves a dual role: aerial combat and ground attack missions with arms ranging from CBU cluster bombs to Maverick antitank missiles.

TSGT ROSE S. REYNOLDS/U.S. AIR FORCE

EF-111R Raven

Loaded with radar-detection and electronic jamming devices, unarmed $73.9-million Ravens—with a range of 2,500 miles and a top speed of 1,400 mph—led the charge into Iraq on the first night of the air war, clearing a path for allied bombers.

TSGT HANS DEFFNER/U.S. AIR FORCE

Patriot Missile

The air-defense missile, a $1.1-million item, made a stunning debut against the Scud, downing forty-nine of the fifty Iraqi rockets it engaged. Flying at speeds up to Mach 3, the 2,200-pound Patriot is guided by ground radar to its target, knocking it out in a burst of shrapnel.

JOHN R. McCUTCHEN/SAN DIEGO UNION

Tomahawk Cruise Missile

Along with laser- and TV-guided GBU glide bombs, these were the first "smart weapons" used in war. Controlled by a ground-mapping computer, the $1.3-million cruise has a 700-mile range and carries a 1,000-lb. warhead. One cruise stopped at a Baghdad corner, hovered, then took a left turn.

U.S. ARMY

AH-64 Apache Helicopter

The U.S. Army's main antitank chopper performed ferociously in the early phase of the ground war, chewing up Iraqi defenses with laser-guided Hellfire missiles and 70mm Hydra air-to-ground rockets. The nimble $11.8-million Apache, can climb at 3,240 feet per minute and cruise at 180 mph.

DOD

M1A1 Abrams Tank

Silencing critics who pointed to its gas-guzzling turbine engine and delicate electronic hardware, the $3.8-million M1A1 proved its worth in Operation Desert Storm, outgunning Iraq's top-of-the-line Soviet T-72 tanks with a 120mm cannon, firing armor-piercing shells.

U.S. NAVY

Night Optics and Satellites

In the allied victory, the eyes had it. With infrared light-amplifying goggles, coalition soldiers could fight at night. They rarely got lost thanks to handheld electronic compasses linked to Navstar Global Positioning Satellites 22,000 miles above the earth.

BOB PROTHERO/ARMY COMMUNICATIONS

Tornado GR-1 Strike Jet

British Tornado pilots took on the dangerous low-altitude attacks against Iraqi air bases early in the air war. The sturdy $36-million jet can carry ninety types of ordnance, including JP-233 antirunway bombs. These containers hold bomblets that crater airstrips and act as antipersonnel mines.

Cinderella Tale

slow, ugly airplane that the Air Force has been trying to junk for more than a decade became the hero of the Gulf. The $8.7 million A-10 Thunderbolt (affectionately called the Warthog) is credited with killing 1,000 Iraqi tanks and 1,200 artillery pieces—almost a quarter of Saddam's inventory.

Obsessed with developing fast fighters, the Air Force belittled the A-10 from the day it began to be made in the 1970s. Almost every year A-10 production money would be shifted to other accounts. But General Schwarzkopf proved to be the shining prince of the Cinderella plane. He ordered the Air Force to assemble 150 Warthogs at a base north of Dhahran.

Pilots from "Hog Heaven," as the base was known, went hunting the Republican Guard one day and destroyed twenty-three tanks with twenty-four Maverick missiles. The last missile proved a dud. Hog pilots also killed more aircraft in this war than all the Air Force's F-15 fighter pilots with their $32 million machines.

The Warthog's prototype was a Luftwaffe dive-bomber fitted with heavy cannons, which was used to perforate the armor of Soviet tanks during World War II. A German pilot, Hans Rudel, who helped develop that plane, was credited with destroying 500 Russian tanks. In the 1960s, Pentagon planners, coming across a book Rudel had written, decided to design a plane around a massive gun, the GAU-8/A. The seven-barrel Gatling, made by General Electric, fires 3,900 rounds per minute.

A captured Iraqi captain told interrogators, "The single most recognizable and feared aircraft by my men was the A-10."

The Calm Eye of the Storm

Far from the thunder of bombs and rockets, but with a life-and-death responsibility of their own, were command posts like the air traffic control center of the USS Kennedy. By the glow of their radar screens, the carrier's technicians run a sea-borne version of a modern airport. Their ultimate task: guiding jet aircraft that have slowed to a hazardous 135 mph to a safe landing on a 500-foot steel runway that is pitching and rolling six stories above the waters of the Red Sea.

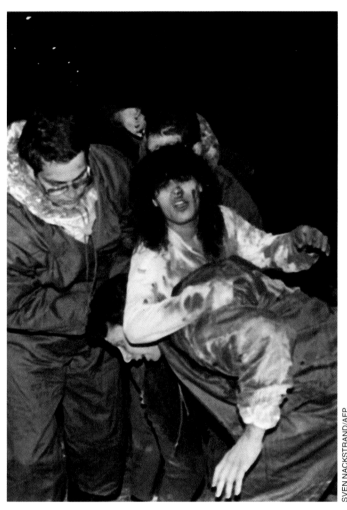

Terror from the Skies

*Soviet-built and Iraqi-modified, the notoriously
inaccurate Scud missile was more potent as a
threat than a weapon of destruction. General
Schwarzkopf said he'd be "more afraid of standing
out in a lightning storm." But while early attacks
on Israel (above and top right) caused little serious
injury or damage, they nearly fulfilled Saddam's
hope to draw Israel into the conflict. After tense
talks, the White House convinced Tel Aviv not to
retaliate. Saudi Arabia's capital, Riyadh, was hit,
too (bottom left). Ironically, one of the last of the
eighty-one Scuds fired did the most harm, killing
twenty-eight U.S. soldiers in their Dhahran
barracks (far right).*

RINA CASTELNUOVO/CONTACT

PHILIPPE WOJAZER/REUTERS/BETTMANN

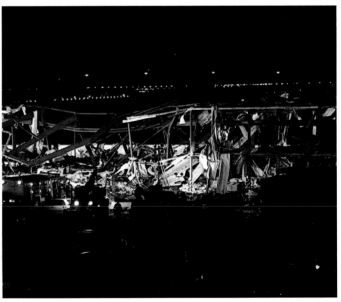
J. SCOTT APPLEWHITE/WIDE WORLD

The Diplomatic Missile

Unassuming in its cratelike launcher, the Patriot air-defense missile was pivotal to the political course of the war. Blowing attacking Scuds out of the sky over Israel (left) and Saudi Arabia, it helped hold together the allied coalition, and won plaudits from the President.

PATRIOT

PROUD
AMERICANS
TAKING
RESPONSIBILITY
IN
OUR

End of the Beginning

The air assault proved the most effective in history. During six weeks of 3,000 missions a day, 90,000 tons of explosives were dropped on the enemy. The total bill for the air war is estimated at $30 billion.

This reinforced-concrete building in the heart of Baghdad was pierced by an allied bomb.

"It Looks Like *Star Wars*"

By Gregory Jaynes

Two weeks into the war, I stood on a berm on the Kuwaiti border, watching the B-52s rumble over, emitting their distinctive double contrails, signing the sky. They had a wingspan as wide as an eighteen-story building is tall. They carried ten times more bombs than any other aircraft in the war—1,000-pound clusters, creators of Vesuvius-sized holes. One day the B-52s dropped 315 tons of bombs; another day, 470. When they detonated, according to Major Dick Cole of the Air Force, it was "like rolling thunder. It's a great psychological effect. You scare the hell out of them." The B-52, said Major General John L. Borling, deputy chief of operations for the U.S. Strategic Air Command, "has a great mystique about it because of its destructive power. It has an ethos, a sense of awesomeness." You could stand thirty miles away from the bomb site, hear the roar, and in seconds feel the hot, meaty breath of it brush against your cheek.

Air war was the word for nearly five weeks. And among the earliest heroes were the crews of the seventy Tornado bombers at work over Iraq. They took the biggest risks, flew the lowest altitudes. Half of them were British, a quarter Italian, a quarter Saudi. They carried 18,840 pounds of airfield attack weapons and their mission was to bomb runways and leave land mines salted generously behind to discourage repairs. "The margin for error is very small," said Group Captain Bill Hedges, detachment commander of Tornado bases in western Saudi Arabia. "Some of the American planes are a mile up. We are flying at 100 feet in the face of antiaircraft fire in darkness.

There is no time to recover." After five missions, Flight Lieutenant Paul Smyth recalled that his "most enduring memory would be of being uncomfortable—I don't know if that's how fear manifests itself." Twelve Tornados went down, and ten British airmen were lost.

Kuwait was on fire, its refineries dynamited by the foe. Standing on the berm you saw an awful black sky. "It's amazing, flying up there," said fighter-pilot Captain Bradley Siepel, an F-111 weapons system officer. "You look at Kuwait, the whole area, it's just fire." At the same time, the B-52s and the F-117 Stealth bombers were robbing Baghdad of power and water. "The most simple things, all the things one took for granted, no longer exist," a Baghdad citizen said. "Even shaving in the morning is impossible. Where do you get the water?" Another Iraqi in the capital said, "Old habits die hard. I still automatically switch on the light switch when I get home. Nothing happens, of course. I still turn on the tap and expect water. Nothing."

Along about here Saddam Hussein took to the radio, accusing allied forces of trying to push Iraq out of the twentieth century, as if Saddam himself weren't stuck in time. Next day, the allies bombed Baghdad twelve hours straight.

More bombs, more missions—60,000, then 70,000, then 80,000 sorties. "Every morning and every evening the sky is full of fire," a woman in Baghdad wrote her daughter in America. "It looks like *Star Wars:* airplanes, jets, rockets, missiles. Every second the house shakes. We get used to the shaking, but not to the being afraid." Another resident wondered pitifully why the bombardment could not cease, saying, "Have they not destroyed everything already?"

What a lopsided war it seemed. "It was as if we had no adversary," said Air Force Captain Genther Drummond, who had a role in the opening assault. But there *was* danger. Flying a combat mission, said Navy Lieutenant Tyler Kearly, was "three and a half hours of boredom and ten minutes of stark terror." Kearly looked out one day and saw eight surface-to-air missiles headed his way. "I saw a flash on the ground and a cloud of sand," he said. "Then I saw a flare go up and I realized it was tracking me. That got my

Gregory Jaynes covered the Gulf crisis for *Life* magazine.

attention. It was pure adrenaline rush."

President Bush counseled early on against euphoria: "There will be losses. There will be obstacles along the way. And war is never cheap or easy." But the fighter jocks could scarcely contain their enthusiasm. One afternoon Captain Ayedh al-Shamrani, an F-15 pilot for the Saudi Air Force, swung in behind two Iraqi Mirage F-1s and blew them away. "I just rolled in behind them and shot them down," he said matter of factly. "It was easy." He's a little guy, short and slight, but his voice had height. "Every pilot I am sure is eager to shoot down an airplane," he said. "It was my day."

By the end of the second week, Americans thought the air war was going so splendidly that eighty-five percent of them expressed confidence in the military, the highest figure in over twenty years. Meanwhile Saddam executed the commanders of his own air force. Taking the hint, scores of his pilots tore off with their planes for asylum in Iran.

In those days before the ground war, a lot of things seemed unreal and farcical. The American military was obsessed with security to the point of silliness, as though Saddam Hussein did not possess a map, much less CNN. Renegade journalists, hotspurs, were moving about the war zone unescorted, playing a dodgy cat-and-mouse game with the authorities and usually getting caught and detained and coming away from it huffy. If you wrote that the pilots seemed giddy, the military censors would change the word to proud. In time people began to ignore Scud attacks, going on about their business instead of putting on their gas masks and seeking shelter (this, though Iraq would launch eighty-one in all against Israel and Saudi Arabia, killing fifteen civilians and twenty-eight GIs, injuring 200, damaging 4,095 buildings). In the Saudi town of Hafar al-Batin, close to the Kuwaiti border, on a Friday after a Scud had leveled a downtown corner, there was no feeling of war. The Al Fao Hotel was quiet except for the sound of a vacuum cleaner on the nubby, torn carpet. A few Syrians at the reception desk tried to ring Damascus. In the street there was only the flip-flop sound of sandals headed for the mosque. In the empty souk, the wares—pots, kerosene heaters, rich rugs—were simply covered and abandoned for prayer. There was no threat of theft. The liveliest citizen of the mud-walled neighborhood was a mongrel dog of about sixteen; it chased its tail to get at a tick.

But the war was real and furious and you could see this in the faces of the Iraqi deserters who straggled across the border at a rate that rose from a trickle of fifteen or twenty a day to thousands. They were hungry and cold and they had been living in dank holes under carpet bombardment. They would strip, throw down their weapons, raise anything white. They came in blankets, barefoot, demoralized. "Thank you, thank you, thank you," they said over and over as their captors gave them food. "God willing," said a young one from Basra, "Saddam will fall and his problem will finish. If Saddam doesn't fall, this Mideast problem will continue. I want to have a special message to Saddam Hussein: He should give up everything. Let's live in peace."

From Kuwait City a civilian reported, "It is like being a caveman to live this way." People were hiding in air-conditioning shafts, anything. Yet morale stayed high, according to a university professor. "With each bombardment," said Fouad al-Falah, "people are saying, God, please save the pilot. Imagine! He's bombing your home, your school, and your country, and you're praying God will give him a safe return."

God didn't always do that. Sixty-three U.S. aircraft were lost. Several pilots managed to survive the excruciating process of ejection. You point your plane "tits up," as the Air Force puts it, and pull the release between your thighs. Feet must be on the rudder pedals and thighs flat on the seat, or else ankles and knees will be broken. Head must be erect and chin pulled in, torso in a straight line, or the neck will snap instantly. A rocket blows you out, and if the force is not greater than the force of the falling plane every bone will break. "The idea is not to watch where you're going," said Air Force Major Bruce Collins. "You are in God's hands."

It cost hundreds of millions of dollars a day to run the air war, and it soon became clear that the enemy would have to be dislodged from the ground, that it was only wishful to think that Saddam, seeing the cradle turned into the city dump of civilization, would back off. Secretary of Defense Cheney and General Colin Powell flew to the Gulf and met for nine hours with the military. In an F-117 Stealth fighter hangar they both wrote messages on laser guided bombs. Cheney: "To Saddam with affection." Powell: "You didn't move it, so now you lose it."

And then: a stutter. On February 13, two bombs dropped by American Stealth fighters struck a building in Baghdad, killing about 300 civilians. The building had always been used as a shelter for civilians, according to Iraq. Not so, said the American military, sensitive as ever about collateral damage, which is to say killing anyone not in service against the allies. For the first time since the outbreak of this war, the world watched as bodies, whole and in part, were fetched from the rubble. Up to now it had been surgical, strictly military, largely off camera. Protests broke out in the streets of Jordan, Yemen, Tunisia, and Sudan.

F-16 star warrior heads for what one U.S. pilot called "ten minutes of stark terror."

———————— ✪ ————————

Two days later, however, hearts rose. Saddam proposed a pullout, then pulled the rug out from his own proposal. He linked it to Israel's withdrawal from the West Bank, the Golan Heights, and southern Lebanon, among other conditions. Bush called it a "cruel hoax." Nonetheless, the gesture was enough to cause jubilation in Baghdad. Soldiers manning antiaircraft guns fired into the air, members of the Popular Army militia let loose a barrage of machine-gun fire and more and more cars were seen in the streets—a remarkable event, considering black market gasoline was then selling for $200 a gallon, or two thirds the average monthly wage.

The bombing continued though, only more terrible than before. As preparation for the ground war, the Air Force let loose 15,000-pound daisy cutters. These so-called poor man's atom bombs sent out a petroleum mist that detonated in the air and became a sheet of fire devouring an area the size of a football field.

In Saudi Arabia, the road to the front—a two-lane blacktop called Tap line—suddenly became unbelievably clogged with allied ordnance moving north and west toward Kuwait and Iraq. There were more than 500 dust-choking miles of trucks groaning with missiles, rockets, boxes of machine-gun clips, trucks bearing tanks and armored personnel carriers, fuel trucks, water trucks, trucks stacked with lumber for latrines and showers. Along the southbound lane came an endless stream of empty trucks returning to take on more. The road quickly became cardboarded, potholed, torn away in patches, its shoulders shorn off by the incredible traffic. And everywhere on its flanks were automobile carcasses, the sheared off, smashed up, turned-into-accordion testaments to the civilian motorists who tried a broken-field run through the convoys and failed. It was, depending on your point of view, either the road from hell or to it.

And the ground war had not yet begun. ☐

Beginning of the End

At 4 A.M. on February 24, the allied ground offensive was launched and ten divisions began rolling deep into the lightly defended Iraqi desert, cutting off Saddam's Republican Guard. In just 100 hours the war would be over.

Tanks crossed the wasteland with astonishing speed—some moving at 45 mph—to surprise the enemy.

Into the Line of Fire

On their way to Kuwait City, marines of the 1st Division Task Force wear gas masks as enemy shells whistle overhead. Saddam never resorted to chemical warfare, but the hot, plastic headgear was in every allied pack. Two filters gave each soldier clean air for twenty-four hours. In Khafji on the Saudi border, marines hunkered down behind a wall for protection.

A Wall of Dust

In the desert, first and last, there is sand. Fine as talcum powder, it gums up everything from rifles to delicate electrical systems. Tank crews wrote home for panty hose to use as engine air filters. Windblown sand stings the eyes and grinds away at helicopter rotors and optical lenses. In a dust storm, troops—like these of the XVIII Artillery Corps—could be stopped blind for hours. Commanders lived in dread of a shamal: 45-mph winds pushing a 100-mile-wide wall of sand. A sandstorm "hits you like a rock," said one U.S. officer. "All you can do is stand in it. There's no place to go."

Erasing All Trace

In southern Iraq, an enemy tank is splattered by sand and heavy debris from a nearby bunker explosion. The blast was triggered by Rangers from the 82nd Airborne Division, who were wiping out Iraqi emplacements. The tank was blown up next.

Women Wore Boots Too

★

Never before have so many American women—32,000 of them—gone to war. Few if any fired guns, but many carried them. They served as ferry pilots, shipboard navigators, tank mechanics, truck drivers, paratroopers, communications experts, ground-crew chiefs. They filled sandbags and loaded heavy gear, sweated, cursed, fought the eternal grit and nursed their blistered feet. Officially, ambivalence followed them to the Gulf. Women shouldn't be this close to battle. Should they? They wore GI pants, yet they were helping to defend a Saudi Arabia that does not allow its women to drive cars or even show their faces. Those who left children back home —some only weeks old—were especially worried. Said one sergeant: "I don't want them calling anybody else 'Mom.'" Eight died, including an Army helicopter pilot, Major Marie T. Rossi. She was buried with full honors in Arlington National Cemetery. Women brought historic change to our armed forces, and—in death—they truly were equal.

The Women

All duties but those on the front lines were shared by the women warriors. Washstands were coed too. But because of customs in Saudi Arabia, women were not allowed to jog, wear shorts, or go shopping—even on the base—unless accompanied by a man. With no television available, conversations took on a new importance. Women make up more than 10 percent of the U.S. military.

HAND WASHING + SHAVIN
ONLY
SFC TORO

JEAN-CLAUDE COUTAUSSE/CONTACT

Each span of twenty-four hours was filled with exhausting work and then sleep. Quarters were in mobile homes, schools, and barracks built by the Saudis. As many as two dozen women were assigned to a room with cots only three inches apart. GI boots, designed with drain holes for jungle swamps, collected sand. Desert-style footwear, ordered up by General Schwarzkopf, was not available until May—well after the cease-fire.

DAVID TURNLEY/DETROIT FREE PRESS/BLACK STAR

ROB TAGGART/REUTERS/BETTMANN

The Women

"I volunteered for the Army, not the Girl Scouts," said one officer, annoyed by the combat prohibitions that limit a woman's advancement. Almost forty percent of military medical units are staffed by women, the largest number in any specialty. At right, Lieutenant Linda McClory of the 5th MASH Unit cares for a soldier wounded by a grenade.

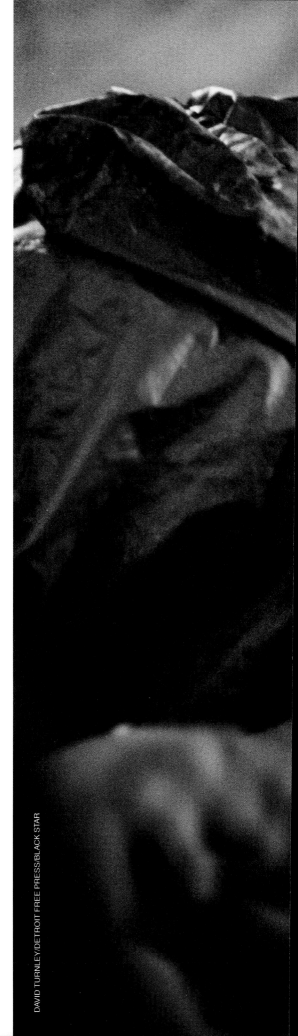

The Story Behind the "Picture of the War"

By Photographer David Turnley

David Turnley of The Detroit Free Press *captured, almost certainly, the most memorable battlefield image (page 22). He recounts the scene:*

A crewman is pulled from the Bradley after it received a direct hit of mortar fire.

I was with the 5th MASH unit. When the ground war started, we were deep in Iraq, just south of the Euphrates. There had been an intense battle between the 24th Mechanized Infantry Division and the Republican Guard.

Our helicopter touched down about a hundred yards from several U.S. Bradley fighting vehicles drawn up together in this vast desert. Battlefields in Iraq were very unlike those in previous wars where one saw two armies actually engage in combat. In Iraq the weapons involved tanks that could kill at very long ranges.

One of the Bradley vehicles had received a brutal hit. The soldiers grouped around were angry and upset. They said it had been struck by friendly fire from a U.S. tank.

The wounded were pulled from the Bradley, and Sergeant Ken Kozakiewicz was rushed to our helicopter with a fractured hand. The medical staff collected the body of the Bradley driver in a bag, put it on the chopper, and handed the driver's identification card to Kozakiewicz. It was only then that the sergeant realized the body in the bag was his friend. This was the moment captured in the photograph.

Then we lifted off and headed back to the medical facility about fifteen minutes away. I didn't speak very much. It wasn't the moment to do that because of the noise from the helicopter, and I felt the men deserved time to deal with the feelings and thoughts they had. I wanted to leave them that dignity. The last thing people need in situations like this is any kind of false affection or anything less than honesty.

In the first place I was physically right next to these guys in the helicopter, so there was no way to feel distant. I had been out there for three months myself, and at some level I probably related to the situation that Ken found himself in. I had made a choice to try to document this war, but I was able to fly in and out, which had not been his luxury, for the last several months. I sort of patted him on the leg at one point, and our eyes met—I did this as a way of getting some sense of how he felt about my being there.

Later I asked the men's names, where they were from, and how they would feel about having their pictures published. They said, "Publish the pictures."

The Pentagon did everything it could to manage the images that came out of this war. It is dangerous to control the public's perception of what the country is involved in. I was there to try to document the realities of war as well as I could.

From the very first moment, this war frightened me more than anything I have ever covered in Beirut, South Africa, China, or Romania. This was a war where human life paled in significance next to the awesome technology being used. The military perception was that the allied losses were light, but that is a very frightening concept—a life becomes a drop in the bucket in a war that involves 800,000 soldiers on one side and half a million on the other. People were going to die—a young man's life passing away in one moment and his body being put into a green canvas bag. This could have happened to anybody.

My fear always was at its worst when I was back in the hotel, contemplating going out to the front with the troops. Once I found myself in their company, my reaction changed. My fear subsided, and I accepted the reality I was in and somehow naturally avoided the worst kinds of thoughts.

One of the real high points of the experience for me was meeting the dozens of American soldiers. Their generosity and strength, sense of humor and love for their families and for their fellow soldiers overwhelmed me, and I really got very much caught up in that.

It was not until a day later, the evening of the cease-fire, that I got back to Dhahran and found that my editors had not received my film. The military officials said, "Oh, yes, we've been holding your film because we feel it's sensitive. There are casualties, and we need to make sure that the next of kin in your frames have been notified." There had been plenty of time to get word to the next of kin. I am especially sensitive to the idea of a family seeing a photo of a wounded relative before they had been notified. But had I not been there to retrieve my film, these pictures might never have been published at all.

After I left Saudi Arabia, I found myself obsessed with reaching the family of Ken Kozakiewicz to find out how he was doing and how his family had reacted to the picture that was published. I spoke to his father in Buffalo. Daniel Kozakiewicz had been in one of the first American units in Vietnam. One of his good friends, the only volunteer in his group, had been killed, so he had gone through a situation similar to his son's. I was concerned that the pictures had been too painful for him and his family, but his reaction was quite different. "They're trying to make us think this is antiseptic," he said. "But this is war. Where is the blood and the reality of what is happening over there? Finally, we have a picture of what really happens in war." A pin had been placed in Ken's hand, and he was back in Fort Stewart, Georgia.

War is a tragic statement about humanity. I would hope that we as human beings can find ways to avoid this kind of thing. I feel that very strongly. □

Sergeant Ken Kozakiewicz, center, is rushed by medics to a waiting chopper.

Medic Clarence Acosta, right, attends Kozakiewicz and Michael Tsantarakis.

A grief-stricken Kozakiewicz learns that the bag holds the body of his friend.

War's Reality Brought Home

*Gayle Edwards, with children Bennett, Adrianne,
and Spencer, hears a mournful taps played in
tribute to her husband, Marine Captain Jonathan
"Jack" Edwards, killed during a flight over
Saudi Arabia.*

Thirsty Fortresses

GIs gave their M1A1s names like "Brain Damage," "Bad Attitude," and "Born to Be Wild." The rolling fortresses cost $4.4 million each, drank 330 gallons of fuel a day, and radiated menacing power. They charged Iraq with 120mm guns booming.

West of the road to Basra, an Iraqi tank bursts into flames after taking a direct hit as the blitzkrieg stormed past.

The Climactic Tank Battle

By John Fialka

It is difficult to imagine how the beginning of the climactic battle of the 100-hour ground phase of the Gulf war must have looked to the handful of guards manning a desolate bunker in Iraq's southeastern desert, twenty miles from the Kuwaiti border. They were the first to see it coming.

Before a dust storm blew up early on Tuesday afternoon, February 26, the land to the south of them was trackless sand, marked only by a few clumps of brush. As the dust began to settle, something resembling the San Diego Freeway materialized out of the haze—ten lanes of very heavy traffic coming right at them.

In front were the boxy Bradley fighting vehicles, thinly armored, tank-like troop carriers equipped with small, stubby cannons. Behind them were the sleeker, more heavily gunned M1A1 Abrams tanks, and behind the tanks were all manner of military vehicles, supply trucks, fuel tankers, vans, mobile command posts. The traffic stretched to the horizon.

Two full U.S. Army corps stiffened by French and British units—some 260,000 soldiers in all—had secretly rolled over seventy miles into the Iraqi desert. Their mission: to surround and eviscerate the Republican Guard. The Iraqis in the bunkers were no fools. They promptly gave up.

Then Colonel William Nash, forty-seven, the cigar-smoking commander of the 1st Brigade of the U.S. 3rd Armored Division, received an order to make a sharp right turn and plunge into Kuwait. Intelligence reports had located the Tawakalna Division

of the Republican Guard in the northern Kuwaiti desert, and Colonel Nash and the division's commander, General Paul Funk, had worked out the details on how to get to them on a map laid out on the hood of a Hummvee, the modern successor to the jeep.

As the sky blackened with thunderheads, the 1st Brigade formed a wedge and headed east. Within two hours, artillery began to rumble and tank main guns began to find their throaty voices.

The baggage train behind the brigade stopped as the evening horizon became dotted with flashes from firefights on three sides. The brigade's scouts had run into Soviet T-72 tanks, one of the hallmarks of the supposedly elite Guard.

With a loud whooshing sound, glowing white warheads of missiles from three U.S. multiple-launch rocket systems arced toward the battles, one on the right, one on the left, and one just a mile or two ahead. The rocketeers were shooting "six packs," packages of six missiles, each missile capable of destroying an acre or more of tanks by scattering lethal little bomblets over and around them.

Above the battles, A-10 Thunderbolt attack aircraft were stacked in several layers, taking turns making strafing runs with uranium-tipped bullets capable of stitching through a tank. In the gathering darkness, the stubby twin-engined planes known in pilots' slang as Warthogs were invisible, but their tracer patterns formed yellow streaks reaching earthward from 20,000 feet.

It was a fantastic light show. Master Sergeant Richard Cox, thirty-four, of Cincinnati, Ohio, sat among the stunned drivers in the baggage column, watching sinister-looking Apache helicopter gunships hover a few feet over the desert as they waited for their moment to move into the battle. Meanwhile, the earth shook with concussions. "He [Saddam] asked for it," said the strapping, six-foot four-inch sergeant, whose job it was to keep the baggage trains moving. "He bit off more than he could chew."

The voice of Colonel Nash rasped on the

John Fialka covers the Pentagon for *The Wall Street Journal.* He spent four months in the Middle East reporting on the Gulf crisis.

---

command frequency, tersely polling his units to make absolutely sure that all of his tanks and armored fighting vehicles were in the clear before he called in an air strike on a column of T-72s. An A-10 pilot begged for the mission, but Colonel Nash gave it to a waiting Apache, code-named "Death Dealer." "Roger," said Colonel Nash, "You may kill them." At one point, one of Colonel Nash's junior officers broke into the command net to argue that the colonel was giving too much of the battle over to air strikes and artillery. "Get a company in there and shoot 'em up. Give them a chance to die!"

Much has been written about how high-technology weaponry won the Gulf war, but parts of this battle were won with adrenaline. Private Frank Bradish, a twenty-one-year-old soldier from Pocatello, Idaho, was in one of the first Bradleys to stumble into the T-72s. His vehicle was hit before it had a chance to fire its wire-guided TOW missile.

As Private Bradish stumbled out of the stricken Bradley, a second Bradley fired its TOW and blew up the T-72. By that time, two of Private Bradish's fellow crewmen were dead. Bradish crawled back in after the other two, who were also badly wounded. Then he found a flare to use to call the medics. Because three fingers of his left hand had been blown away, he tucked it under his arm and pulled the cap off with his teeth. When help arrived they found him back inside the smoking Bradley, trying to remove the machine gun ammunition so that it wouldn't explode and further injure his friends.

"They had to pull him out of there," recalled Lieutenant Colonel John Kalb, his commander. "Only then did he look down and notice that he was covered with blood." Colonel Kalb said Bradish would be nominated for one of the Army's highest awards for bravery under fire.

For forty-two hours the battle continued, as the 1st Brigade plowed through almost an entire division of the once-feared Iraqi force. Maps recovered from an Iraqi command bunker show that the Republican Guard had elaborate plans to cope with an attack from the south, and had arrayed their tanks, artillery and mines to force the allies into "killing fields" where they would have been slaughtered by artillery. But as it turned out, the Iraqi artillery couldn't shift quickly enough to cope with an attack from the west. "A lot of those tanks were shot from the rear," said Colonel Nash, who kept his armored columns moving throughout the following day and into the night to keep Iraqi forces reeling.

The battle turned nastier Wednesday night, when the brigade had to thread itself through a giant sand dune that housed a complex of Iraqi bunkers, then a mine field and more bunker complexes. Seen through the thermal-seeking electronic eyes of M1A1 tanks, the battlefield was swarming with "hot spots." A lot of them were Soviet T-62 tanks, maneuvering in the darkness. But some of them were haplessly grazing camels whose mutilated bodies were found the next day.

By this time the brigade was too close to the Iraqi forces to safely resort to air power, so this phase of the battle was left up to men like Sergeant Glen Wilson, twenty-seven, of New Haven, Ohio, an M1A1 gunner. At one point during the fighting, his driver was yelling at him to shoot at a tank on his left and his loader was shouting that there was another Iraqi target on his right. "It was real confusing," recalled Sergeant Wilson, who had positioned his gun halfway between the two targets when another tank, a T-72, materialized right in his sights. It was one of five tanks Sergeant Wilson destroyed.

The 3rd Armored Division, the most tank-heavy unit in the U.S. Army, came to Saudi Arabia from Germany, where its mission was to guard the most likely place for a Soviet invasion, the Fulda Gap, on the old border between East and West Germany. Because Soviet tanks outnumbered U.S. tanks, the M1A1 was designed to maximize U.S. tank-killing power with a special computer-driven gun stabilization system that allows the tank to fire accurately at night, while on the move.

The division's tank gunners spent most of last year practicing for the initial battle of a war with the Soviet Union, often using electronic simulators of the tank turret. They work just like video games, and the training proved itself in this battle. "If they [the Iraqi tanks] were moving, we were able to pop them off with no problem," explained Sergeant Wilson.

By midnight Wednesday, Iraqi units were swarming all around the brigade, some of them fighting, some of them looking for a way to give up. Colonel Nash devised a tactic that he had never tried before. He sent some of his Bradleys and M1A1 tanks back to guard his baggage train and then he put a line of M1A1 tanks right up with his scout vehicles to prevent any more surprises like the one Private Bradish had run into. "I call it marching fire," explained the colonel, who added that if he had had enough fuel that night, "I could have gone to Baghdad."

In the rear, Sergeant Cox was among those who struggled to keep the baggage train moving, threading the 550 vehicles one at a time through an eight-foot gap in a mine field marked only by two small, green-glowing Chemlights. Most drivers heeded his instructions to follow in the tracks of the vehicles in front of them, but one didn't, swerving around and then disappearing in

Knots of confused Iraqi prisoners of war—many of them men from the same Guard units that had swaggered in to loot and rape Kuwait—sat numbly inside hastily formed circles of concertina wire. They stared at the Americans, talked quietly, and devoured packets of the Army's new field rations, called Meals Ready to Eat, which the Americans were only too happy to get rid of. It turned out that the Iraqis had never been given orders to attack. "They have been shelled so much they were ready to give up," said Captain Tom Lewis of Windber, Pennsylvania, after talking to

JOHN FIALKA

Master Sergeant Richard Cox, a wagonmaster on the fifty-seven vehicle supply train for the 1st Brigade, named his Hummvee "The Sixth Floor" after he received a care package addressed "to any serviceman," from college girls in a sixth-floor dorm.

---- ✯ ----

an orange ball of flame. It was only an anti-personnel mine, and the driver spent the next few hours cursing because all four tires and the oil pan of his Hummvee had been blown off.

At dawn Thursday morning, the situation became clearer. The desert floor around the Iraqi bunkers was littered with pieces of plastic and aluminum strips from U.S. missiles. A-10s and Apaches had found the Guard units, thoroughly working them over before the brigade got to them. Around 8 A.M., after a night of explosions and constant start-and-stop, the mile-long train halted. Soldiers sat in silence as the news of the cease-fire of the ground war to liberate Kuwait came over their shortwave radios.

some of them.

By noon on Thursday, four hours after the devastating 100-hour attack, the final mopping-up operation was producing the war's last big visual display. The desert sky was filled with orange fireballs as hundreds of captured tanks and ammunition bunkers filled with Soviet-made Sagger missiles and other unused antitank weapons were blown up. The burning Soviet tanks made a sound like popcorn popping as their turrets blew off and the shells and machine gun ammunition inside sent tracers whistling in all directions.

The surviving Iraqis watched, shivering in the sand as the wind prepared to kick up another dust storm. □

Marines Go Rolling Along
1st Division Task Force marines spread across the horizon as they grind into Kuwait in their AAV-7A1 troop carriers. Each twenty-three-ton vehicle—there were more than 400 in action—carries twenty-five men and a 12.7mm machine gun. The carriers are amphibious, a feature of little use in this war.

Blasting 'em Out

During the advance through eastern Iraq, British infantry encountered surrendering enemy soldiers. Two Iraqis in one emplacement hung tough and had to be routed by a sergeant in the 4th Armored Brigade, hurling a phosphorous grenade.

The Road to Ruin

On February 25, Saddam ordered the retreat from Kuwait City. His army packed its plunder and fled north toward Basra. B-52s and gunships pounded the nighttime rout. By dawn, a haunting highway of corpses and smoking hulks was all that was left.

Surrender and Retreat of a Broken Army

BY COLIN SMITH

Some thirty miles north of flag-waving, gun-happy Kuwait City, along the main desert highway to Basra, Iraq's second-largest city, there were low and persistent multitonal humming noises in a place where little else moved except the more adventurous human scavengers. It was the sound of engines still idling in vehicles abandoned intact by the panic-stricken children of Saddam's mother of all battles.

Allied aircraft had arrived as they tried to flee back home with their loot and their weapons. When I got there, around midday on Thursday, February 28, a few hours after offensive operations had been suspended, spot flames still flickered from shredded tires despite a steady drizzle from a sky made even darker by the black smoke from burning oil fields. Ghastly islands of charred bodies and metal were surrounded by more or less intact trucks and cars carrying the riches of Kuwait. The convoy seemed more gypsy than military.

Nothing was too big or too small for the conscript army of peasants and workers who had been brought up in a state that preferred tanks to Toshibas. On the bed of one truck was a complete imitation-leather living room set, large gray metal filing cabinets, and a restaurant's soft-drinks refrigerator with its Canada Dry sticker still on the back. Television sets and VCRs were commonplace, as were soap powder and bottles of after-shave lotion. A chandelier spilled out of its cardboard box. A live

chicken picked around packets of Dunhill cigarettes, a woman's handbag, pieces of costume jewelry, and strings of imitation pearls.

There were a great many new women's and children's shoes. An American officer told me he had even seen a steam radiator: "I suppose it was going back to some little village in Kurdistan where they were going to hook it up to the log fire." He was the commander of an Abrams tank group, part of the Army's Tiger Brigade. Some soldiers from the Tiger Brigade were picking around the wreckage looking for Kalashnikov rifle bayonets as souvenirs. Several hundred weapons, perhaps more judging from the amount of shooting in the air in Kuwait City since liberation, had been taken by the Kuwaitis before the Americans got there. Others concerned themselves with more practical matters. Further down the road, before the last American checkpoint, the

Abandoned vehicles, including this wayward tank, littered the highway to Basra.

citizens of the Middle East's richest oil state were busy siphoning gas or examining roof racks and the beds of pickups for the greatest prize of all—full jerry cans.

Scattered about were the kinds of personal mementos carried by homesick sol-

Colin Smith, the London *Observer*'s defense correspondent, has reported on more than twenty wars. He is the author of *Carlos: Portrait of a Terrorist*.

diers everywhere. One snapshot, near the body of a man lying face down with a terrible wound in his right leg, was of what appeared to be a children's birthday party. The children, three girls and a boy in party hats, sat around a table laden with food and dominated by a heart-shaped cake.

Some broken bags contained blank children's exercise books and German coloring crayons. In one truck the radio had been knocked out of the dashboard but was still wired up and faintly picking up some plaintive Arabic air, which sounded so utterly forlorn I thought at first it must be a cry for help. The next day, American medics did in fact find one grievously wounded Iraqi in the back of a van.

Helmets, gas masks, and ammunition, including grenades and a few plastic mines that the rear guard may have intended to throw in its wake, lay everywhere. A burned-out quadruple-barreled antiaircraft gun, detached from the pickup that had been towing it, pointed skyward and looked as if it might have been returning fire. There was no sign of its crew.

What occurred here and elsewhere was undoubtedly one of the most terrible attacks on a retreating army from the air in the history of warfare. It must surely rank with Israel's destruction of Nasser's forces in the Sinai Desert in 1967 and what the Allies did in 1944 to Hitler's Panzer divisions at Normandy's Falaise gap.

Vehicles sat on both sides of the four-lane highway heading north. More were just off the road out into the desert on the right where they had become stranded after their drivers obeyed some mob instinct to get off the tarmac. There they bogged down in a colossal traffic jam. The sand had been turned into a quagmire by recent thunderstorms. At this point the survivors must have run off into a night that was being torn apart by explosions and flame. They most likely became a part of the sea of allied prisoners of war, or perhaps were still wandering in the desert, too terrified to give themselves up.

Bombs and cannon fire from allied planes were not the cause of all of the wreckage. Traveling in the dark, without lights, some of this fleeing mass of traffic had simply collided with each other in their eagerness to get away. Several vehicles, including an ambulance, had trapped themselves on a wire-net fence on the side of the road. One tank crew had tried to cross the steep central divide only to discover there are limits to where even a T-62 can go. The Soviet behemoth lay tilted there at an awesome list, its hatches up, the crew's blankets and clothing strewn about it.

In those places where the bombs and the 30mm cannon fire at 4,200 rounds a minute came down, the carnage was terrible. Huddled under one highway overpass, like an animal sheltering from a storm, was a burned-out fuel tanker whose driver appeared to have been cremated in his cab. Most of the nearby vehicles had also caught fire, although a new-looking armored personnel carrier not far away was quite undamaged, its crew apparently deciding they would soldier no more.

Many allied troops still seemed to be in almost as big a state of shock over Norman Schwarzkopf's blitzkrieg as the Iraqis. "I wouldn't even call this a mopping-up operation," said one bewildered captain of the 1st Battalion, 5th Marine Regiment, encountered on Kuwait City's seventh-ring road on Wednesday morning. At that point the marines had stopped advancing in order to allow the Saudi and Kuwaiti elements in the coalition forces to take the city. A considerable barrage of small-arms fire was coming from over the brow of a hill, but this turned out to be Arab soldiers firing in the air in celebration.

The marines' last encounter with the enemy had been the previous evening, when they knocked out two tanks and an armored personnel carrier with their own M60 tanks and some wire-guided TOW missiles. "Some of the Iraqis left their vehicles and hid in a nursery—you know, a place where they grow young trees," the captain said. "Two battalions went through and finished them. They didn't fight much, but at least they died with their weapons in their hands."

Now the men of the 1st Battalion's Alpha Company were getting out of their gas suits, having just had the last alert of the war. The marines looked grimy but cheerful. Alpha Company had taken part in the storming of the second breach made in the Iraqi earthwork defenses in southern Kuwait. They said they had had some resistance from a dug-in T-55 tank (a very old armored vehicle), but their own M60s had finished it off. Then they started taking prisoners.

"We used to say that we wouldn't take prisoners unless they came out barebutt and waving a white flag," said Lance Corporal George Cadiente, "but, oh man, some of

them were crying. One guy, you know, he defecated himself. When they heard we were marines they were certain we were going to kill them. They'd been told all sorts of bull like to join the Marine Corps you had to kill one of your own family first. Some of them wouldn't come out of their bunkers. They were curled up in there and wouldn't come out. We'd throw stones in, pretending they were grenades, and they still wouldn't come out. They'd just curl up some more. And the place was full of guns, grenades, RPGs. They could have fought us. When we tied their hands with the plastic strip some of them were saying, 'We love you, we love you.' I had one kid who couldn't have been more than sixteen. He just sat there on the ground and started crying. He was convinced I was going to kill him. He hadn't eaten for days, you could see it. Just a kid."

Lance Corporal Cadiente, of San Jose, California, was twenty-two.

The Iraqi attempt to tow artillery equipment to safety was foiled by allied attacks.

A near-riot had taken place at a U.S. Marine temporary POW camp about forty miles southwest of Kuwait City when some 3,500 half-starved Iraqi soldiers fought each other for American combat rations. Mass hysteria broke out. At one point the marines were throwing cardboard boxes, full of "Meals Ready to Eat," much despised by American troops, over the barbed wire and watching the Iraqis tear them apart. It was like feeding a flock of birds.

Each box of MREs contains at least two

pork dishes—pork patties and ham slices—but in their hunger none of the Muslim captives seemed to notice. "Meester, Meester," they implored as the Americans approached with the food, each man definitely an island.

The mood of the Iraqis' guards varied from intense irritation to great compassion. "Poor bastards. You can't even dislike them. All you can do is feel sad for them," said Captain Kurt Snyder, a bespectacled law graduate from Seattle, who said he was there because he did not know anyone else who had read all of the Geneva Convention.

Even as MPs were screaming obscenities at their prisoners in the manner of very young men trying to be very tough, U.S. Navy medics were helping an Iraqi doctor treat the sick and wounded. The Americans fussed around them, attached intravenous drips fixed to poles in the ground, asked people to search for extra blankets, and pleaded with their officer to arrange for a helicopter evacuation to the nearest MASH unit, which was duly done. One young Iraqi, gray-complexioned and obviously in great pain, had a wound right through one ankle and injuries around his groin. But the medics treated only two men for battle injuries. They said the rest were suffering from dehydration, and thought that this was partly brought on by fear. One stretcher case was shivering so badly he looked as if he had an acute attack of malaria. Others had shown scars they said they had collected in the Iran-Iraq war. "Basically they just want some attention, want to know that somebody cares," said Navy corpsman David Walden, twenty-one, from Columbus, Ohio.

As dawn broke on Monday, a photographer and I had been flagged down on a Saudi border road by forty very scared Iraqi soldiers waving white rags and undershirts, in one case tied to a broken-off radio antenna. They carried pathetic little bundles of food—tomato paste and dried biscuits. They were concerned that they might still be attacked from the air and wanted motor transport to be arranged.

It was only after we crossed into Kuwaiti territory that the full disintegration of Saddam's army could be seen. As we approached what was to become the marines' POW camp, a great black phalanx of broken men was shambling toward it. They looked as if they might have stepped out of a painting of Napoleon's retreat from Moscow. These were the lucky ones. □

Scenes from Hell

The desert of Kuwait was a grim and grimy waste-land in the aftermath of the swift ground war. Twisted and charred weapons littered roadways, and it took new tire tracks to reveal the clean sand beneath the mire of gooey oil soot. Thousands of Iraqi troops, bypassed in the haste of the land offen-sive, wandered the countryside, and some had yet to lay down their arms. "They don't seem to have figured out," said a U.S. general, "that they don't have an army anymore."

BRUNO BARBEY/MAGNUM

Then Came Quiet Chaos

U.S. forces rounded up an estimated 60,000 Iraqi troops. "We are not afraid," said a surrendering Iraqi soldier. "We are just tired of war." Indeed, the land itself seemed tired of conflict. The smell of death hung in the air over endless miles of destruction. A U.S. pilot involved in the final attack described the scene as "close to Armageddon." And it was.

Among the Other Victims

Desert wildlife—the most innocent of the creatures caught up in the tide of battle—may suffer the most. Far from a barren place, the desert is an abundant, but delicate, ecosystem. The environmental toll exacted by the fighting and pollution from burning oil wells is incalculable.

The Vanquished

The piteously outstretched hand of the incinerated Iraqi soldier was a symbol of the devastation where death came by remote control. Most of the defenders were glad to surrender even though some half-expected to be shot as prisoners. The victors, were, of course, ready instead to feed them and tend their wounds.

ERIC BOUVET/ODYSSEY/MATRIX

TODD BUCHANAN/PHILADELPHIA INQUIRER/MATRIX

Their Fighting Was Over

In makeshift camps like this one in northern Saudi Arabia, enemy prisoners were interrogated. By the third day of the ground war, 5,000 Iraqis already had been processed and transferred by the 503rd Military Police Battalion to Saudi government supervision.

End of the Trail

As the cease-fire was being negotiated, these trucks were hit; the footprints of the fleeing enemy surrounded the convoy.

Freedom Rolls In

The Iraqis had fled, and the allies arrived unopposed. Fearful that the embassy was booby-trapped, U.S. troops landed on the roof—an eerie mirror image of Vietnam.

WELCO

ME TO KUWAIT

كويت

Wrapping Up the Victory

U.S. special forces (far left) helped mop up specific pockets of resistance in the city where 80 percent of Kuwait's population of two million had lived before the war. Collaborators were collared (left, bottom) by the sixty-odd resistance groups that operated during the occupation. U.S. troops, who had diplomatically let Saudi and Kuwaiti columns liberate the city, quickly got to join in the cheering.

PASCAL GUYOT/AFP

The Rape and Rescue of Kuwait City

By Michael Kelly

he city the Iraqis left behind when they fled Kuwait appeared to have been worked over by a huge army of drunken teenage vandals. They had stolen everything they could, from air conditioners to cigarettes, in a city-wide smash and grab. The huge and superb medical library at the city's teaching hospital, Mubarak al-Kabir, was stolen in its entirety. So was the library at Kuwait University, along with the school's big mainframe computers and everything else worth a cent. Standing near the library, where a few thousand bedraggled books *(Henry the Fifth, The Italian Renaissance and Its Historical Background*, etc.), along with hundreds of thousands of index cards, remained scattered on the floor, Omar Samman, an eighteen-year-old student, described the looting: "They came in with lorries and took everything—the computers, the books, the carpets, the chairs, the keyboards, the carrels, the microphones, the podiums. It took them nearly a whole month, with men in lorries every day, before they got it all."

What the Iraqis could not steal, they destroyed, in an astonishingly savage and thorough rampage. They torched every major hotel, the banks, car dealerships, almost every store in the downtown shopping district, a score of major office buildings, the fishing marina and all its boats, the National Museum, and a great deal more. They ruined the beachfront with lines of concertina wire, bunkers, pillboxes, and mines, and turned Gulf Street's luxury apartment buildings into high-rise bunkers, cinder blocking the windows into gun ports. They shot up and burned down the Emir's office and residential palaces, as well as the parliament building, smashing the windows and doors and breaking the furniture.

Kuwaitis were stunned by the Iraqi soldiers' habit of turning every place they went into a sty. At Kuwait University every office, it seemed, was ankle- to calf-deep in debris; the contents of desks and files dumped on floors, paintings ripped from walls, chairs and tables overturned. In one room was a great pile of gold- and azure-trimmed academic robes, sodden and stinking of urine. At the Al-Ahadat police station, which the Iraqis converted into one of many makeshift prisons, as many as 200 men were locked in one thirty-by-thirty-foot room, with no beds or blankets. The prisoners slept on a filthy tile floor and used scraps of Styrofoam for pillows. As elsewhere, the Iraqis' own living quarters in the prison contained layer on layer of grime; half-eaten, rotting plates of food flung into corners, trash and garbage covering the floors, graffiti on the walls, the stench of feces and urine heavy in the air.

It is the human factor that hurt most, though. The Iraqi forces treated the people as they did the property. They trashed them. "They killed the people and threw their bodies in the dirt," said District Attorney Nassar Seleh. "They killed the people like they were chickens."

Abdul Rahman al-Awadi, Kuwait's minister of state for cabinet affairs, claims that 33,000 people disappeared after August 2. The Iraqis are reliably estimated to have taken as many as 20,000 prisoners to Iraq to serve as slave laborers, and another 3,000 to 5,000 as hostages and shields in the days just before the allied ground offensive. By the minister's reckoning, that would put the number of murdered between 8,000 and 10,000. This figure is improbable, but not wildly so. The dead were everywhere.

In a cemetery in the southern suburban district of Rigga, mass graves, each reportedly containing seven or eight men or boys, stretched for long rows. Cemetery workers said the slots contained about 1,000 bodies. There are ten major hospitals in Kuwait City, and all report having handled atrocity victims. At Mubarak Hospital, one of the city's largest, the chief of surgery, Dr. Abdullah Behbehani, said that from late

Michael Kelly was *The New Republic*'s special correspondent in the Gulf.

August through October his emergency room received groups of five to ten corpses almost every day. At the Al-Amiri Hospital, Dr. Sabah al-Hadeedi said he can document, with photographs and fingerprints, thirty-eight executions.

Drs. Behbehani and Hadeedi charted, in the precise way of professional accountants of casualties, the patterns of death. The first pattern is chronological, with the execution of civilians beginning several weeks after the August 2 invasion, in response to resistance efforts, and drastically increasing from mid-September on, after Saddam Hussein's brother-in-law, Ali Hassan Majid, arrived as the new governor. Majid reportedly brought in squads of trained killers from the Iraqi state security agency, the Mukhabarat. "The executions began in earnest after they sent in the execution squads from Baghdad," said Dr. Behbehani. "We started seeing a lot of young men between the ages of seventeen and thirty-two. They arrived, not as patients to care for, but as bodies to bury."

The second pattern is one of style, identical in almost every case. After arrest, a victim would be imprisoned and interrogated for several days or weeks. Upon release, sometimes secured with bribes solicited from the family, the prisoner would be returned home and shot in the head, neck, or heart, in front of family members. Alternatively, his body, with ankles and hands bound, would be deposited near his home. The families were generally barred from retrieving the bodies from the street or doorstep until the next day, so that many might see them and fear.

The third pattern was one of even worse brutality. "There started in late September something more severe. We started getting mutilated and tortured bodies. Not simply shot, but eyeballs taken out, heads smashed, bones broken," said Dr. Behbehani. "You would see heads that were completely unvaulted, with no brains in the skull, or multiple fractures in each arm, or severe burns in the face and body, or fingernails removed.

"The signs of torture I saw from the thirty-eight executions this hospital handled were electrical burns, where wires had been put on the chest wall and near the genitals, and cigarette burns anywhere on the body, massive bruising, and nonlethal bullets in the shoulders, kneecaps, hips, and legs," he said. At about the same time, the doctors also began seeing more cases involving women, often raped and mutilated before death. "In November a woman I know personally was brought in," Dr. Behbehani recalled. "The top of her head was gone and bullets were in her chest." Sitting at his desk, a neat, polished man reflected in a neat, polished surface, the doctor wept. "She was—my God—she was completely mutilated. There was no brain inside her skull. Why should they take her brain? Why do such a thing?"

Rape and torture not resulting in death were also common. A few days after the liberation, a man handed me his business card, which said he was Bassam Eid Abhool, assistant electrical engineer at Kuwait International Airport. His fingernails were perhaps one eighth of an inch long; tiny, soft, fragile little strips of ragged cuticle. "Ah, you see my fingers," said Abhool. "Iraqis, of course." His story was typical: picked up at random walking in his neighborhood; taken to a police station; hung upside down naked; beaten, tortured, interrogated; released with a warning. Much of the questioning was political. "They would say, 'You know what your Emir do for your people? Marry 200 women and take all your money —is this not true?' I would say, 'I don't know.' They would say, 'The Iraqi people have come to give freedom to people of Kuwait; is this not true?' I would say, 'I don't know.'"

There was real resistance here, and it was never completely overcome. Dr. Hadeedi and his colleagues entered wounded resistance fighters into the hospital as car accident victims to fool Iraqi watchers and hid an entire fifty-bed ward and operating theater in three basement storerooms. Five-person resistance cells worked in a loose food and money distribution network that provided those in need with staples and cash every week. Some people fought with arms up to the end, despite an Iraqi policy of collective reprisals that meant half a dozen Kuwaiti deaths for every Iraqi death. A favored tactic was to invite a lonely Iraqi soldier home to dinner and at evening's end stab him and bury him.

But for most people here the seven months were mostly a time for hiding. The postliberation boasts of opposition were often about how the rich hired cranes to put their Ferraris on their rooftops, how every neighborhood was stripped of street signs and house numbers, how valuables were secreted in backyards and young men in cubbyholes.

The release from captivity took the form of that most pleasant of releases, a party. The bash began unexpectedly, early in the morning of February 26. "We woke up and saw the Kuwaiti flag flying from the police station," said Nassar Seleh. "You cannot imagine our feelings when we realized that Iraqi troops had gone from the city. In the night we had heard the tanks moving in the street, and we had dared hope they were going. But to wake up and find all of them gone—the city is ours again!"

Suddenly everyone was a rebel. The streets were filled with young men firing rifles and pistols, making the celebration almost as dangerous as the battle for liberation itself. Early reports cited six such

The Kuwaitis liberated after seven months of occupation were ecstatically grateful.

deaths in the first two days; I know of three, whose fresh graves I visited in Sulaibikhat Cemetery. ABDULLAH JASSIM, WHO DIED FOR KUWAIT, read the headstone of a man hit on top of the head by a falling round.

At Al-Amiri Hospital a long line of cars lined up to take souvenir shells from an Iraqi antiaircraft gun, and families posed for pictures next to it. In a heavy rainstorm four young women sat in a row on the trunk of an Impala, having made a seat by knocking out the rear window. They waved to the crowd like princesses, and yelled over and over, "I am Kuwaiti! I am Kuwaiti!"

For Americans the party offered the novel sensation of being adored in a foreign land. An American couldn't pay for anything that week in Kuwait, couldn't walk ten feet without being stopped to accept thanks, couldn't talk to anyone without getting an invitation to dinner or lunch. "Welcome, soldiers, you are welcome," three little girls serenaded the U.S. Marines at the newly reopened American Embassy. "George Bush, very, very, very, very, very, very, very, very, very good," an old man offered. Two women jumped from a car to proffer a daisy and a tray of cookies. "Thank you! Thank you! And thank Mr. Bush," said one. "Welcome to your country," said the other.

At one raucous do, centered on three Kuwaiti armored personnel carriers whose crews stood unusually erect in the manner of young men posing for posterity, four teenage girls wearing sweaters covered with photos of Bush, John Major, and Margaret Thatcher (each framed with little red and gold and silver spangles) worked the crowd of American soldiers and reporters with their autograph books. I wrote, self-consciously, "To Maha, on a wonderful day, 3-1-91," under an inscription from a Captain Henry Douglas: "To a lovely Kuwaiti girl."

There were few Iraqis left in Kuwait City against whom retribution could be exacted. But five days after liberation I drove up the road toward southern Iraq, the route Saddam's soldiers had taken in flight. Every fifty or one hundred yards there was a fresh kill from the slaughter the allied forces visited on the fleeing Iraqis. From each charred and trashed vehicle the belongings of the dead Iraqi driver and the dead Iraqi soldier-passengers were spread in a dirty plume on the asphalt.

Most of the bodies had been carted away, but a fair number remained. At every spot where there was still an Iraqi corpse, a crowd had gathered. Every few minutes a new group would approach, and someone would pull the blanket down to see the enemy's face. The corpses were already decomposing, their faces yellow and black and green, their features melting together under a buzzing of flies. One by one the Kuwaitis moved cautiously forward and paid their last respects. One middle-aged man bent down over half of a machine-gunned body wedged upside down in the driver's seat of a stolen Toyota. He spat, carefully, on the face. His friend got it all on videotape. They pulled the blanket back up and got in their car, heading up the road to spit on the next of the waiting dead. □

SANTIAGO LYON / REUTERS / BETTMANN

شكرًا لـقوات الـتحالف.

Thank you For Every Thing

الصامدون

Happy Days Are Here Again

Those who endured the Iraqi's staged a joyous, ragtag parade just as soon as the invaders melted away. Three days later, on February 28, U.S. Ambassador Edward Gnehm, Jr., ran up the Stars and Stripes at the embassy. There was still shooting in the streets, but this time it was in celebration.

MICHEL LIPCHITZ/WIDE WORLD

A Tale of Two Leaders

In Kuwait, where the Emir returned to his throne, promising democratic reforms, angry citizens raged against the man who demolished their country. In Iraq, Saddam's mighty image was shattered. His armies decimated, Saddam faced violent uprisings and U.N. demands that he pay for the war he caused. Bidding to become the supreme Arab statesman, Saddam had only succeeded in destroying his land.

RICHARD ELLIS/REUTERS/BETTMANN

Badge of Courage

Celebrations saw somber moments, as Americans remembered those killed and injured in the line of duty. Lying on a gurney, wounded Staff Sgt Daniel Stamaris, a freed POW, salutes the flag at Andrews Air Force Base near Washington.

Sweet H

MARK PETERSON/JB PICTURES

Home Again

After months of boredom and tense days of battle, the first troops came back to an ecstatic heroes' welcome. Members of the 24th Mechanized Infantry arrive at Fort Stewart, Georgia; a Navy flier hugs his wife and child.

Lessons of Victory

Peter David on the legacy of a brilliant military and political performance

Benjamin Franklin said there never was a good war, or a bad peace. From the point of view of America and its allies, the war in the Gulf was a good deal better than most. It was over mercifully fast—in less than six weeks from beginning to end. Its cost in allied lives was lower than even the rosiest forecast produced by the Pentagon had dared to suggest (the total number of American, British, and French deaths was a little over a hundred). A lot of things that could have gone wrong didn't. Iraq did not use chemical or biological weapons; it did not even use the fuel-air explosives that America used against it. Despite Saddam Hussein's provocations, Israel did not join the war and so detonate a wider conflagration. In no Arab country did the people respond to Saddam Hussein's pleas to overthrow their governments and turn against the United States. The Soviet Union did not come to the help of its former ally. Above all, this was a war in which the moral issue was clear: Saddam Hussein was wrong to invade Kuwait, and he was evicted by armies that went into battle with the full legal and moral authority of the United Nations.

This happy outcome owed a good deal to luck. Saddam Hussein invaded Kuwait at a moment when world politics were in flux. Had he done so five or even three years earlier the chances are that the Soviet Union would have warned the Americans against a military intervention. That would probably have made George Bush's decision to rush American forces to Saudi Arabia a good deal harder, and it would certainly have sunk the hope of fighting a war under the banner of the United Nations. If the Warsaw Pact had not disintegrated in 1989, the United

Bush walked to work early on the morning the bombing began.

States might not have dared to transfer to the Middle East such a big chunk of the army it had sent to defend Europe. Luck was important in many smaller ways, too. If the Scuds falling on Israel had killed hundreds of civilians, Israel would certainly have entered the war. Had Saddam Hussein seized one of the many opportunities he was given to withdraw without a fight, his war machine might still be casting its shadow over Iraq's vulnerable neighbors.

Still, to meet a challenge like the one in the Gulf, good fortune on its own is not enough. A full accounting of the Gulf war and the events that preceded it has to acknowledge that the United States was blessed during this crisis with political leadership of the highest quality. George Bush had never looked like a particularly strong or decisive president. He was thought to be deficient in the "vision thing." Yet for some reason of character or biography, he grasped at once what was at stake in the Middle East. Another president, weighing the imponderable dangers of facing down Saddam Hussein, might well have decided that the deletion of Kuwait was something the world would have to adjust to. From that first fateful weekend at Camp David, however, Bush made it clear that he had chosen the other path. There would be no Vietnam in the sands of Arabia, but there would be no Munich either. Iraq would have to withdraw empty-handed from its conquest or face war with America.

Could Iraq versus the United States have ended with anything other than victory for the superpower? Once it came to war, certainly not. But simply in order to give himself a credible military option, Bush had to deploy formidable political skills. He had to win over fainthearted King Fahd, persuade Mikhail Gorbachev to stay on the sidelines, steer a dozen resolutions through the Security Council, maintain a balance between America's Arab allies and its ties with Israel, squeeze billions of dollars out of the Germans and Japanese, and convince a timid American Congress that stopping Saddam Hussein was worth the price in American blood. Even when all this was

One of the legacies of the war is a severely damaged ecosystem.

done, and the battle had been joined, other tests remained. Bush had to resist the pressure from those who wanted to start the land campaign before the bombing had done its job, and from others who wanted the bombing to go on indefinitely. In this decision as in so many others he seemed to get the balance approximately right.

Saddam Hussein, in contrast, got virtually every decision he made exactly wrong. When he invaded Iraq he misjudged the response not only of the United States but also of his supposed friends in the Soviet Union and the Arab world. By seizing thousands of hostages he made it easier for the United States to rally world opinion against him—then let them all go once the damage had been done. He let his near-victory in the war with Iran delude him into thinking that he could stand up to a coalition of some of the world's most modern armies, with a superpower at their head. Toward the end of the bombing campaign and when the land war had just begun he issued a stream of bewildering and contradictory orders that sapped whatever remained of his army's will to fight.

Beyond the brilliant personal performance of America's

president there lies a bigger question about what the victory in the Gulf is going to mean for America itself. In the first flush of success the meaning seemed plain enough. For all its economic woes the United States was still the one true superpower. The economic collapse of the other military superpower, the Soviet Union, gave the Americans unprecedented freedom of maneuver in both the United Nations and the Middle East. The United States of Europe, that superpower-in-the-making, spent much of the crisis demonstrating its disunity. The other economic superpowers, Germany and Japan, were meanwhile neither able nor willing to take part in the military operations against Iraq. Because they reluctantly supported Bush's decision to go to war, however, they felt obliged to join the Gulf Arabs in becoming the war's main paymasters. Indeed, one of the most astonishing features of the war in the Gulf is that for two of its main participants, America and Britain, the economic cost may turn out to have been zero.

There is nothing like a great military victory for imparting false lessons—military lessons as well as political ones. In particular, Americans should not believe that the war against Iraq means that future wars against small or medium powers will be equally bloodless on the American side. For all the brilliance of General Schwarzkopf's one-hundred hour land campaign, history is likely to concur with the judgment of America's air-force chief of staff, General Merrill A. McPeak, that the Gulf war was the first in which air power inflicted a decisive defeat on a field army. By the time the land war began, which means by the time allied soldiers were put in harm's way, the war was virtually over. Although estimates vary, it seems clear that somewhere around 100,000 Iraqi soldiers in and around Kuwait were killed by allied bombing before G-Day, which is more than a thousand times the number of deaths the Iraqis managed to inflict on the Americans over the same period. So it is scarcely surprising that, once the land war started, large chunks of the Iraqi army—perhaps most of it—simply decided not to shoot back.

These circumstances will not readily repeat themselves. When again, in the Middle East or anywhere else, will the United States have convenient bases, a host of allies, and five leisurely weeks in which to bomb a com-

GREG ENGLISH / WIDE WORLD

pletely friendless adversary into near-submission? During this war, moreover, Saddam Hussein turned military incompetence into something akin to an art form: a modern air force of more than 600 Iraqi aircraft did not launch a single attack on an allied ground unit, an army of thousands of tanks did not launch a single effective counterattack. All he could do was set fire to Kuwait's oil fields and pour millions of barrels of polluting oil into the northern Gulf. In the next war the enemy's army and air force may fight instead of flee, and may be armed with night-vision equipment and cruise missiles of its own. The wider international environment of some next war could also be starkly different. It is hard to imagine another big military clash in which the Soviet Union will be happy to give the United States a free hand, on which the permanent members of the United Nations Security Council are entirely united and for which a lot of affluent nations not directly involved are nevertheless willing to pick up the tab.

After the Second World War a victorious United States occupied Germany and Japan and later saw both countries flourish under democratic governments. Victory in this war, too, gave birth to hopes of a prosperous and peaceful future for the Middle East. It is no reflection on the execution of Operation Desert Storm to say that most of these hopes are liable to be disappointed. America and its allies were right to go to war against Saddam Hussein, both to liberate Kuwait and to stop a ruthless despot from putting a chokehold on the world's oil-driven economy. His vicious repression of his own rebellious Shiites and Kurds in the weeks of internal unrest immediately after the war was over shows just how dangerous leaving him master of the Gulf would have been. Many of the difficulties of the Middle East, however, are too deep-seated to be healed by a few months of nimble diplomatic footwork.

In much of the region it will take years for all the consequences of this war to make themselves visible. For the Arabs the war ushered in a period of bitter self-questioning. The Iraqi invasion of Kuwait turned their world upside down, shattering in one blow generations of fine words about Arab unity and brotherhood. Yet Arabs outside Iraq are partly to blame for what happened on August 2. It was they—not the West—who did most to build Saddam Hussein into the monster he became. Before August 2, Arabs had basked in what they considered the reflected glory of the Iraqi army. When Saddam Hussein inflicted a near-defeat on Iran, in a war he himself had started, his Arab neighbors hailed him as a saviour. When he dropped cyanide gas on his own Kurdish citizens, other Arabs (including Kuwaitis) turned a blind eye, and then rebuked the Americans for daring to com-

plain. Before invading Kuwait, Saddam Hussein hung a journalist from Britain, threatened to burn up half of Israel, bragged about his chemical arsenal. Instead of restraining him, the Arabs cheered him on.

Some Arabs, notably the Palestinians and the Arabs of North Africa, continued to cheer even when he was destroying Kuwait and torturing its people. For others, however, the war threw a harsh light on the flaws of the Arab world and stripped away many illusions. The flaws include, almost everywhere, the absence of a democratic or even moderately accountable government. Saddam Hussein posed as a popular Arab hero but was exposed in the war's aftermath as a ruthless tyrant reviled by most of his own people. The illusions include the conviction that Israel is to blame for every blot and blemish in the Arab world. For half a century Arab leaders have used fear of the Zionist enemy as a way to divert attention from their own failures and errors. In this war, however, the Iraqi dictator's fiction that he invaded Kuwait in order to liberate Palestine was simply too preposterous to believe. Firing his Scud missiles at Tel Aviv was a way for Saddam Hussein to ask his Arab brothers a difficult question. Can you

Days after the fighting stopped, graves were still being dug.

Iraqi refugees continued to seek haven.

be against me, if I am so clearly against Israel? To his surprise, and perhaps to theirs as well, the rulers of Saudi Arabia, Egypt, and even Syria—the self-proclaimed "beating heart of Arabism"—answered "Yes, we can."

Because some Arab governments chose to answer this way, the American victory in the Gulf has raised hopes that it might be possible to end the Arab-Israeli conflict itself. During the war, countless editorialists in Europe and the United States wrote high-minded articles about the need, once Kuwait had been liberated, to resolve the Palestine question, which was, they insisted, "the underlying cause of instability in the Middle East." This, alas, may be little more than a pious hope. Israel is one of the causes of instability in the Middle East. But if this war proved anything it proved that it is not the only cause. Saddam Hussein would have invaded Kuwait whether the Jewish state had existed or not. Meanwhile his attempt to turn Israel into a scapegoat resulted in millions of Israelis, including many survivors of the Holocaust, having to sit night after night under missile attacks waiting fearfully for poison gas. For most Israelis the war was proof that the desert region in which they live is still a jungle, in which surviving depends on owning the sharpest pair of claws. Persuading Israel to give up "strategic depth" on the West Bank and Golan Heights so that the Palestinians who supported Saddam Hussein can have a homeland is necessary, but it is going to be fearfully hard.

Throughout history, military victories have been followed first by relief and then by disappointment. The people of America and Britain and all the other countries that contributed to the victory in the Gulf should not allow the inevitable disappointments to cloud their final judgment about the war. It was not a war that ended all wars. It will not necessarily be a war from which a harmonious "new world order," or even a peaceful Middle East, automatically springs. The tragedy in Kurdistan put paid to that illusion. It was, however, a necessary war, which righted an obvious wrong and stopped a bloodthirsty tyrant in his tracks. That is reason enough for pride.

The editors and publisher wish to thank

ROGER AILES   PEGGY ALLEN   ANDY AMBRAZIEJUS   MAGGIE BERKVIST   GREGORY CERIO
COLLEEN WINDERL COHEN   CONDÉ NAST PUBLICATIONS   TERESA CRAWFORD   COLIN DAWKINS   WILLIE DESIR
GENERAL MICHAEL DUGAN   JOAN DWORKIN   LESLIE ESSER   CAMPBELL GEESLIN   LAURA E. GIARDINA
LISA HARTJENS/IMAGEFINDERS, INC.   MITCHELL IVERS   LINDA KAYE   MIKE KENTZ   MARY MAGUIRE   ELIZABETH MATT
JAMES MEACHAM   DOROTHY O'KEEFE   DAVID PARADINE TELEVISION   JOYCE PENDOLA   LINDA RICE   DIANA RIGGLE
KENN RUSSELL   FRED SAMPERI   ELIZA SMITH   JUSTINE STRASBERG   COLONEL HARRY G. SUMMERS
ALISON CARB SUSSMAN   MERCY VAN VLACK   HARRY WACHENHEIM

PETER DAVID is the international editor of *The Economist* of London. A Middle East specialist who has traveled extensively in Israel and the Arab world, he was responsible for all aspects of his paper's coverage of the Gulf story.

RAY CAVE, formerly the editorial director of Time Inc., was editor of *Time* magazine for eight years. Under his direction *Time* won more photojournalism awards than any magazine in the world. It also received the prestigious American Society of Magazine Editors awards for General Excellence and Design.

PAT RYAN was editor of *People* magazine for five years and *Life* magazine for two. During her tenure, *People* and *Life* won three American Society of Magazine Editors awards, including ones for General Excellence and Design.